SINAI
the Site & the History

SINAI
the Site & the History

Essays by

Morsi Saad El-Din
Gamal Mokhtar
Fouad Iskandar
Gawdat Gabra
Samir Sobhi
Ayman Taher

Photographs by

Ayman Taher, Luciano Romano

New York University Press

New York and London

Page 2:
A satellite camera focused on the "Triangle of Grandeur" illustrates Sinai's ancient role as a natural corridor between the Nile Valley and the Middle East.
(Photo by U.S. National Aeronautics and Space Administration.)

9 8 7 6 5 4 3 2 1

Library of Congress Cataloging-in-Publication data
Sinai : the site & the history : essays / by Morsi Saad El-Din...[et al.] ; photographs by Ayman Taher; Luciano Romano.
p. cm.
ISBN 0-8147-2203-2.
1. Sinai (Egypt) — Pictorial works. I. Saad El-Din, Morsi.
II. Taher, Ayman. III. Romano, Luciano
DS110.5.S493. 1998
953'.1 —dc21 97-29825
CIP

Editors: Gareth L. Steen, Anthony J. De Nigro
Consulting editor: Dr. Morsi Saad El-Din
Project coordinator: Sherif El-Ebrashy
Design: Franco Maria Ricci
Art director: Laura Casalis
Photography: Ayman Taher, Luciano Romano
Color separations: Fotoincisioni Bassoli
Printed in Hong Kong by Oceanic Graphic Printing

Published by New York University Press

2nd edition produced by Words at Play Editorial & Creative Services

Note: Since there is no standardized spelling in the English translation of many ancient or Arabic words, each author has used his preferred spelling in most cases.

Photo credits:
Page 2 — U.S. National Aeronautics and Space Administration;
pages 8-79, 84-87, 115, 116-142 —Ayman Taher;
pages 81, 83, 89, 90, 92-97, 99, 102-109, 111-113 —Luciano Romano

Table of Contents

Introduction: The Splendor of Sinai

by Dr. Morsi Saad El-Din

I must admit, albeit with chagrin, that when I visited Sinai in June 1993 it was the first time I had set foot on the soil of that great peninsula. Nor was I alone in this negligence. Dr. Zahi Hawas, one of our leading Egyptologists, confessed to the same omission. Here we were, two who claim to be intellectuals, and we had never before been in the part of Egypt that has been the passageway of civilization over the millennia. Moreover, I would venture that the majority of Egyptians are guilty of the same neglect.

The visit was quite a revelation, not simply because of the beauty of the scenery, the richness of the mountains, the vastness of the panorama and the abundance of the colors, but also because during my short visit I was able to see, firsthand, the history of that precious section of my country.

Sinai, of course, has always been holy ground – a cradle of religions that played exceptional roles in both antiquity and in recent history. I listened to the saga of Moses's Exodus and saw the place where he received the Ten Commandments, which became an ethical code for the world. I walked parts of the Way of Horus, the ancient military corridor marched by armies since the 15th century B.C. The same road was used by Qambis, king of Persia, when he invaded Egypt in 528 B.C., and by Alexander the Great in 333 B.C. It was the path of the flight of the Holy Family and the route used by General Amr Ibn El-As, commander of the Arab armies that brought Islam to Egypt. It was also the route the Crusaders followed in 1117, and again in 1146 and 1153. The Turkish Sultan Selim I trod this path in 1517, and Napoleon later used it for his expedition to Syria in 1799.

Over the millennia, Sinai has inspired many artists, writers, travelers and holy men of several religions. In his book *The Martyrs*, for example, French author François de Chateaubriand wrote about Sinai, though he had never visited it himself. Sinai was the refuge for Christians when they were tyrannized by the Roman Emperor Maxentius. And Sinai played a pivotal role in the legend attached to the Monastery of St. Catherine. I say legend since historians have not agreed about the authenticity of the account. The Christian Emperor Justinian, so the story goes, built a church in Sinai in A.D. 545 that he named for the Virgin Mary. Catherine was a girl from a noble Christian family in Alexandria, where a large number of Egyptian Christians lived. She supposedly converted large numbers of people and tried to persuade Emperor Maxentius to embrace Christianity. Instead, he ordered that she be tortured on the wheel. When this failed to break her, he had her beheaded. Afterward, Christian monks moved the girl's body to Mount

Opposite page:
The acacia tree, often standing alone and solitary against a barren landscape, is the most common vegetation of Sinai.

Sinai and buried it in the Church of the Virgin Mary, renaming it for the young martyr – St. Catherine.

The legend has survived, crossing over to Europe in the 8th century; and although the Roman Catholic Church dropped her from its liturgical calendar in 1969 because of doubts about the story, Catherine's memory is still revered. There are many other stories associated with Sinai – fact and fiction – which show that it has always been a source of inspiration to many.

To most Egyptians, the Sinai Peninsula, that triangle squeezed steadfastly between Africa and Asia, was until recently almost an alien land. Very few Egyptians visited it, apart from the officers and soldiers of the Frontier Corps who were billeted in El-Arish. It was only after its loss in the 1967 war that a new awareness and appreciation of Sinai was born. In fact, it was this very awareness in the 1973 war that inspired Egyptian soldiers to victory.

It was this same awareness that gave birth to the idea of producing this book about Sinai, a book written by Egyptians as an encomium to a part of Egypt previously neglected.

The second chapter of this book deals with geography – not just land elevations, mountains, valleys, green areas and desert, but geography as a factor – and an important factor, at that – in shaping the national character. Sinai can claim a contradiction: It is both isolated from and closely linked to the motherland. Sinai was always a buffer and protector. It was often referred to as the graveyard of invaders. It was a route for successive waves of armies and therein lies the contradiction. From the Egyptian point of view, Sinai was always a shield against invaders. It did not always stop them, but it invariably resisted them.

The general feeling about Sinai was that it was almost a foreign region or a no-man's-land at best. When the Israelis occupied Sinai in the 1967 war, they inadvertently ensured that never again would Egyptians feel estranged from Sinai. The issue was no longer just Palestine; now a part of Egypt had been occupied. I have always claimed that this is what gave the Egyptian soldiers the stimulus and courage to cross the Suez Canal. It was the feeling that for the first time they were fighting for their own land.

With the return of Sinai after the hostilities, it suddenly became an integral part of the motherland. Memories began to be revived of Sinai as a lively route of caravans, armies, missionaries, Muslim pilgrimages to Mecca and Christian pilgrimages to Jerusalem.

There is, no doubt, a strong relationship between geography and environment on the one hand and traditions and culture on the other – each enforces certain behavioral attitudes. In Sinai, one can also distinguish between two basic geographical features, the coast and the desert. Sinai constitutes 6 percent of the area of Egypt, and yet it claims 29 percent of Egypt's coastline.

It is mainly in the coastal regions that one finds towns and settlements. Consequently there are two disparate vocations in Sinai: animal breeding and grazing in the desert and agriculture and fishing in the coastal areas. Agriculture depends mainly on rains and subterranean waters that accumulate from the rains. Since rains are irregular and unpredictable, subterranean water is the trusted source for irrigation. It is during the *El-Sayl*, or heavy rains, that water accumulates in the wells. The rains are also a factor in bringing change to land features when summer's arid valleys become winter's green fields. This water game, if one may call it that, has created an agricultural heritage of wild plants, palms, olives and cacti that can withstand the arid season.

And what of Sinai's inhabitants? It is difficult to put them in the mould of the Egyptian character. In fact it is wrong to assert that there is one "national character" for any nation. And it is the same with Sinai. The character, culture and identity of the Bedouin people of Sinai are different from the Nile Valley dwellers. The Bedouin have their own morals, traditions and manners. Their isolation from the Nile Valley, precarious as it can be, helped create among them a strong sense of belonging, first to the tribe and then to the region, and a certain pride and self esteem. These kinds of relationships impose certain forms of laws and behavior on the people.

In the vastness of the desert, the Bedouin have honed keen senses of direction and pathfinding that have become part of their lore and their character. In fact, in the pursuit of drug smugglers or other criminals, it is often the Bedouin pathfinder from Sinai who helps the soldiers of the Frontier Corps track down their man. The monotony and the similarities of the scenery have taught them to notice the slightest change in the landscape. One finds that the concepts of time and place are interwoven and that distance is measured by units of time. A Bedouin says a place is half an hour away, for instance, not a kilometer or two.

But these concepts are now evolving as a result of education and communication, and a more sophisticated attitude is emerging. This change has been accelerated by two factors: the Israeli occupation and the culture shock it brought, and the opening of the area to tourism. Visitors from all over the world have brought with them different cultural attitudes that contribute to changes in Bedouin customs and morals.

The natural environment also has helped to define manifestations of social life, especially population distribution. On Sinai's northern coast, for example, stretch several well-established towns and villages whose inhabitants are fishermen by trade. In contrast are the nomads who still pitch their tents where green patches can be found to graze their cattle, sheep and goats. The Egyptian Government is now settling in newly built villages some of the populace who are willing. However, many want to build their own houses – spacious, and with a courtyard. Most people need open spaces for their social gatherings around coal braziers, where they converse, discuss and settle problems. But, unfortunately, few can afford to build their own.

The isolation in which the Bedouin live has also helped to shape their attitudes. It has created in them a sense of belonging to the tribe. The tribe is the source of authority, and its laws govern their whole society. The Nile Valley is alien to them and they refer to its dwellers as *Misryeen*, which means Egyptians, as if they themselves are not Egyptian. They have pride in their history and their traditions. Indefatigable people, both men and women work from early morning until "the shadow of the stick disappears," as the saying goes, at sunset.

Then they all roll in and sit around their braziers, men and women together, to eat their dinner, which is the main meal. Afterwards, over rounds of tea, they recount their news of the day.

The open desert created among the inhabitants of Sinai a love of life and freedom. A Bedouin believes that the whole land belongs to him. He knows the

Following pages:
The austere, sand-filled Wadi Ghazal sits along the route from Nuweiba to St. Catherine's Monastery.

desert like the back of his hand. The Bedouin of Sinai consist of numerous tribes, each with slightly different characteristics in clothing, hair styles, manners, customs and the like.

During a visit to El-Arish in northern Sinai for example, I went to the marketplace and was impressed by the different ages of the sellers. On inquiring, I discovered an interesting fact: the elders of the tribe are responsible for dealing with gold, silver and semiprecious stones; the men between 30 and 50 years old sell vegetables, fruit, livestock and utensils; the women sell homegrown vegetables and fruits, cotton threads, poultry and milk products; and young boys and girls run around and help mind all the different stalls.

Despite modern transport that has invaded Sinai, the camel still rules supreme among the Bedouin. As Samir Sobhi, a writer and artist, writes in another chapter, the camel is the center of life in Sinai and is valued as highly as – if not higher than – humans. It takes the visitor only a few seconds to realize this. A young Englishman who spent an academic year in Egypt studying Arabic observed that while the Egyptian peasant tends to treat his donkey with utmost contempt, the Bedouin on the other hand "revere their camels with a respect bordering on that reserved for the sacred cow in India." Even in the late 20th century, the camel is still indispensable for the nomadic Bedouin of Sinai, providing milk, hair for tents, and above all transport over difficult terrain of mountains and *wadis*, or valleys.

The Bedouin of Sinai originally came from the Arabian Peninsula more than 500 years ago, and they now constitute the majority of Sinai's population. Generally they can be divided into two main sectors – Northerners and Southerners. In the North, with its soft, undulating sand dunes, the tribes still retain the classic black wool tent of Arabia, whereas in the South, with mountains rising 9,000 feet around St. Catherine's Monastery, the Bedouin live in ramshackle huts made of discarded corrugated iron and local plant life. Those who live in the interior raise livestock, mainly goats and camels. On the coastal expanse, however, fishing provides sufficient livelihood for the inhabitants.

Dr. Fouad Iskandar deals with geography not simply from its physical side, but also as a political and economic factor in shaping people's lives. He likewise writes about the future development of the peninsula that began with the return of Sinai to Egypt. In the past, Dr. Iskandar claims, Sinai was used to pass into and out of Egypt. It was a kind of transit station for trade and armies. Due to its geographical features, people were reluctant to settle down there – or even to set foot on its soil. Hence the prevalent feeling among Egyptians that Sinai was an alien land, isolated from the mainland and just an arena for armies to fight in and a gateway for invasions. Even in modern times, Dr. Iskandar points out, four rounds of wars were fought there between Egypt and Israel.

Following the 1973 war, the Egyptian Government initiated a new policy that encouraged integration with the motherland. That policy is based on the assumption that Sinai is part and parcel of Egypt and not simply some kind of shield, or a buffer zone used only during time of war. Such a policy is not easy to carry out for a number of reasons. The most important is the inhabitants themselves, who will always be reluctant to change. Changing an attitude is difficult, of course, and cannot be attained overnight. For both the inhabitants of Sinai and the dwellers of the Nile Valley, it needs to evolve as a spiritual and mental change as well. There is a dire need for a complete overhauling of the social, economic, and political structure. As Dr. Iskandar puts it: "Thus, a new era in the history of Sinai began in October 1973. The peninsula has become an integrated part of Egyptian territory. Sinai is no longer reserved for military purposes; it is open to all Egyptians, the same as all other parts of the Republic."

Sinai's history is dealt with in this book by Dr. Gamal Mokhtar and Dr. Gawdat Gabra. Their two chapters are complementary, but whereas Dr. Mokhtar explains history in secular terms, Dr. Gabra traces the history of religion as practiced in the peninsula. These aspects are two sides of the same coin.

History books often deal with the lives of kings and emperors, but both Dr. Mokhtar and Dr. Gabra deviate from this. They give us the history of the people and their beliefs over the millennia. Dr. Mokhtar begins with an explanation of the name of Sinai and its derivation. "What is in a name?" Shakespeare asks in *Romeo and Juliet*. In the case of Sinai, it matters a great deal. There are many theories put forward, but as Dr. Mokhtar puts it, despite the role of this peninsula in Pharaonic history, "we have not, until now, been able to ascertain a definite, consistent name that the ancient Egyptians gave to Sinai."

Pharaohs sent expeditions there in search of gold and turquoise, but its name changed from dynasty to dynasty. When they went in search of turquoise, they called it *Mfkat* (pronounced mif-kat), which means the Land of Turquoise. The famous Harris Papyrus of the 20th Dynasty (1188-1069 B.C.) refers to Sinai as the Turquoise Country. In fact, the peninsula was given the name of every precious or semiprecious stone that was sought after. Sinai, with its mines, was always rich.

The first archeological dig in Sinai, Dr. Mokhtar tells us, was by a British archeologist named Francis Lewellyn Griffith. But it was Sir Flinders Petrie, known as the Father of Egyptology, who undertook excavation on a scientific basis in 1901. His shovel first fell on Maghara and Serabit El Khadem, which Dr. Gabra fully explains. The results of the excavation proved, beyond any doubt, that Pharaonic expeditions went after the riches of the Sinai mines. But it was turquoise that overshadowed all other ores.

Among the Pharaohs whose names are associated with Sinai was Senefru, founder of the 4th Dynasty. But inscriptions in Maghara show that ancient Egyptian expeditions covered the whole of the Old Kingdom (2700-2190 B.C.) up through the 12th Dynasty (1991-1785 B.C.). Remains of a temple honoring Hathor – who was called "Supreme Goddess" and "Mistress of Turquoise" – have been found at Serabit El Khadem. Built at the time of the 12th Dynasty, that temple was probably the only place of worship in Sinai then; its aim is believed to have been to protect the mines, ensure the success of production and, according to Dr. Mokhtar, "to bring a sacred dignity to the place."

Dr. Mokhtar also brings up an interesting and controversial point: the temple was later used for Semitic religious practices and sacrifices by the Bedouin tribes. The evidence includes timber ashes, two conic stones in the temple, and the remains of basins and tanks that might have been used in the ablution ceremonies.

Following page:
Near Ras Mohammed, constant winds off the Red Sea sculpted a crevasse in Wadi Khashabi over the millennia.

Copper was also mined by ancient Egyptians. King Ramses III of the 20th Dynasty (1186 - 1154 B.C.) was the last great Pharaoh to order the mining of copper. Inscriptions reveal that both mining and smelting took place.

Dr. Mokhtar summarizes the historic battles fought in Sinai which, during the 2nd Dynasty (2925-2700 B.C.), was regarded as a hostile area with uncivilized inhabitants. In fact, the kings of Egypt during that period continually fought to bring the people of Sinai under their rule. Later, during the First Intermediate Period (7th to 11th dynasties), weakened by internal political strife, her rulers tried to establish peace with the inhabitants of Sinai. Later still, Sinai witnessed the invasion of the Hyksos and they occupied most of Egypt. They were eventually defeated at the hands of Ahmose I in what is now the Gaza Strip.

The Way of Horus on Sinai's northern coastal strip is certainly among the most ancient and important military routes in the world. Dr. Mokhtar describes this strip that became the mainland bridge used by invading armies. It was also the trade route between Egypt, Africa and Asia. All along the Way of Horus, forts were built, as were supply centers for water and food. The route was first used by Qambis who commanded the Persian army when it invaded Egypt in 528 B.C. In 332 B.C., Egypt was invaded by Alexander the Great, who was helped by the Egyptians themselves. Then came Christianity, when the Egyptian Church became the center of national resistance against the Byzantine Empire. In A.D. 640, the Arab commander Amr Ibn El-As crossed Sinai and easily invaded Egypt. Dr. Mokhtar relates the findings of several excavations carried out by both foreign and Egyptian missions.

Dr. Gabra carries on where Dr. Mokhtar ends, and examines the Sinai's historic role in three of the world's great religions. Dr. Gabra calls the peninsula "the crossroads of three religions, Judaism, Christianity and Islam." This ecumenical and pivotal role is reflected by a project proposed by the late President Anwar el Sadat, but never built, for a rest house in Sinai flanked by a synagogue, a church and a mosque. Sinai is also associated with the Exodus, which is mentioned in both the Bible and the Koran. According to the Koran, Moses went to Mount Horeb where he lived for 40 years. There he found the solitude and tranquility he needed to meditate, and it was there that God revealed Himself to him in the miracle of the Burning Bush.

The route that Moses is believed to have taken with the Israelites became a holy place for Christians as well as Jews. At the different stops that Moses made, people began to pursue hermitic and monastic life. From Christianity's earliest times, hermits began to seek solitude in the same sites where Moses had led his people. It was also through Sinai that the Holy Family undertook their flight into Egypt, along the coast of the Mediterranean.

Sinai was also the route through which the Arab armies under the command of Amr Ibn El-As came to Egypt, bringing with them the message of Islam. It was from Sinai, via the Nile Valley, that both Christianity and Islam spread to Africa and Asia. What is more, it was the peninsula that became a transit point for trade to the Far East. It was likewise through Sinai that the pilgrims trekked on their way to Mecca and Medina. The pilgrims' route was also used to take the Mahmal, an Egyptian gift of silk, to Saudi Arabia to cover the Kaaba.

Dr. Gabra gives detailed

descriptions of the Pharaonic temples built in Sinai by the ancient Egyptian kings. The most famous is the Temple of Hathor at Serabit El Khadem mentioned earlier.

Dr. Gabra describes the temple's murals that show the king making offerings to Hathor, protector of the turquoise mines.

Dr. Gabra discusses the controversy over the route taken by Moses during the Exodus. While no one questions the authenticity of the event, which is mentioned in all the Holy Books, the route it took has always been debated. Another debatable issue is the number of the Jews who were led by Moses. Dr. Gabra believes that the figure of two million is highly exaggerated, and from different documents he estimates the number at about 27,000. It is interesting to note that there is little mention of the Exodus in ancient Egyptian texts, which indicates that it was given little importance in Egypt. But there is a text from the time of Pharaoh Merenptah (1212-1202 B.C.) that describes Israel as "lying desolate." By the same token, there is no certainty as to the identity of the Pharaoh who oppressed the Jews. The names of Merenptah or his father, Ramses II (1279-1212 B.C.), and Amenhotep II (1425-1401 B.C.) or Amenhotep III (1390-1352 B.C.) are usually mentioned.

Dr. Gabra devotes a good part of his chapter to the Monastery of St. Catherine. One point he stresses is that the Arabs never interfered with the monastery or its inhabitants. During the Arab rule, 641 monks continued to live there, "unmolested and unscathed." He relates how a delegation of Christian monks went to meet the Prophet Mohammed in A.D. 625 to ask him for protection. Mohammed granted the famous *Achtiname Testament* that protected them from danger and exempted them from taxation. A copy of this document can be seen in the monastery today. The original was taken away by the Ottoman ruler Sultan Selim I along with many other Egyptian art works. The *Achtiname Testament* underlines the tolerance and respect of the Muslims for the monks of St. Catherine and for the monastery itself.

The library at St. Catherine's Monastery claims 4,000 manuscripts, about 3,000 of them in Greek. There are several hundred texts in Arabic, Syriac, Gregorian, Armenian, Coptic, Ethiopian and even Slavic. The library also has about 5,000 books, some of them dating back prior to the printing press.

St. Catherine's also boasts one of the world's richest collections of icons, representing some of the finest works of the early Byzantine period.

The monastery is not the only Christian monument in Sinai. There are a number of churches and chapels, as well as Muslim tombs and mosques. Many of the art works in Sinai were transferred to Israel during its occupation of the peninsula, but with the return of Sinai an agreement was reached to return the works to Egypt.

In spite of the existence of so many ancient monuments, excavating is still going on, undertaken by both Egyptian and foreign missions, including one from Japan. These digs have uncovered many interesting monuments and historical objects that will certainly add further information about the historic, archeological, religious and cultural role of Sinai through the ages.

Taken together, the five chapters, written by experts in their respective fields, give a comprehensive picture of Sinai. But what about the present? Not a

Following pages:
The high plateau of Serabit El Khadem, almost inaccessible and uninhabited, was the site of turquoise and copper mines and the ancient Temple of Hathor, whose ruins are still visible, during the Middle and New Kingdoms (1895-1074 B.C.).

day passes now without reading about all kinds of development projects in Sinai. Perhaps the motherland feels some kind of guilt as a result of the years of neglect and nonchalance it displayed towards Sinai. But since its return to Egypt, many projects have been carried out in two important fields: infrastructure and tourism.

The government has already realized two five-year plans for Sinai, the second from 1987 to 1992, and the third is nearing completion. The main objectives of these policies are to permanently end the isolation of Sinai from the Nile Valley; to exploit water resources to the fullest, be they from the Nile, rains or underground wells; to discover untapped sources of ores; to build up industries near the sources of raw materials; to redistribute Sinai inhabitants among the new housing settlements; and last but not least, to develop tourism.

Already a number of projects have been completed, especially in the areas of agriculture, industrialization, fishing, tourism, education, culture, information and housing. The main push has been on infrastructure: water and water purification, electrical supplies, drainage, communication and transport.

Construction of the Ahmed Hamdi Tunnel beneath the Suez Canal underscored the need for a physical link with the mainland. The tunnel is 5,913 meters long, with 1,640 meters under the canal itself. For the first time cars can go directly from the west bank to the east bank of the waterway without having to use ferries. A 1,700-kilometer highway system has been built to link Sinai's various parts, thus ending the long tribal isolation.

It is in agriculture, perhaps, that the greatest strides have been made. Large areas have been reclaimed from the desert and are now in full production. The main crops are olives, palms, nuts, apricots, guavas and all kinds of vegetables. Commercial fishing has also been developed and makes full use of both the sea and Lake Berdawil. This lake is the largest of the Bitter Lakes and is rich with fish. Refrigerated trucks now transport fish directly to the markets of Cairo and other cities in Egypt, and it is now common to hear Egyptians talk about high-quality Sinai fruits and fish.

Although Egypt has exploited mineral resources for many years, a new policy of prospecting for oil and other ores is now afoot. New oil deposits have been discovered and old unused mines are being reopened. New factories to process ores, such as ferromagnesium and gypsum, have been built. And high-quality marble compares well with international production standards. Other materials now being produced are coal, sulphur and natural gas. Even the sands of the Sinai are being put to work since they contain 98.7 percent silicon oxide, which is used to make glass and solar cells that can produce heat and generate electricity. Geologists expect to find other valuable ores like dolomite and phosphate.

Other important products found in Sinai are the medicinal plants that grow naturally in the desert. Pharmaceutical tests show these products can help treat respiratory illness, stomach and digestive troubles, skin diseases, rheumatism and other ailments.

Perhaps most remarkable of all is Sinai's emergence as a center for tourism. After the 1967 war, there was a rush to build villages and hotels; and even during the recent seasons in which tourism was badly affected by terrorist activities in the rest of Egypt, resorts were busy in Sinai.

The land offers a variety of

attractions, and the whole peninsula can now be reached through a number of bus and air services. The diversity has sparked three forms of tourism: cultural, religious and recreational. For culturally minded tourists, the government is developing an open-air museum at Maghara that would contain 12th Dynasty artifacts found in the area that are now housed in the Egyptian Museum in Cairo. Also proposed is a museum for the first alphabet known to man, at Serabit El Khadem. Other attractions include the Citadel of Sallah El-Din (or Saladin, as he is known in the West), built between 1183 and 1187, and the Citadel of El-Tor built during the reign of Sultan Selim I.

Religious tourists visit the holy area between Wadi Feran, Surial Mountain and Moses Mountain, or Mount Sinai, where historians believe Moses received God's message. They also follow the two routes mentioned earlier that Moses traveled, the route of the Exodus and of the Mahmal.

Sports enthusiasts and naturalists enjoy flora and fauna, as well as sailing, fishing and diving along 150 miles of coastline with black mountains as a backdrop, and vast beaches and spectacular offshore coral reefs at Aqaba and Sharm el Sheik. The coast, particularly in those areas, has attracted a plethora of hotels and diving clubs offering complete tourist amenities. Tourists can also learn to hunt with trained falcons, a new attraction that is an ancient practice among Arabs. And if they overdo in all of this, they can take to the recuperative sulphuric springs at Pharaoh's Baths.

This is Sinai today, a land that is both young and old, a land that, like the biblical Prodigal Son, has come back to the family fold and has been met with open arms and an open heart. Sinai is also the land of the future, a land to be discovered and rediscovered, as this book intends to assist in doing.

Bedouin women of the Mazeinah tribe of South Sinai in traditional dress.

The History of Sinai

by Dr. Gamal Mokhtar

Sinai is many things. It is the corridor between two of the earth's largest and most culturally rich continents, Africa and Asia; it is the land bridge between Egypt and the Levant; it is the meeting point of civilizations since prehistoric times and the crossroads of epic human migrations and wanderings.

Sinai is the land of the Proto-Semitic alphabet, the mother of alphabetic scripts; it is the repository of scattered rock inscriptions in hieroglyphics, Nabataen, Hebrew, Greek, Latin and Arabic that recorded and narrated history's events and dramas.

Sinai is the protecting shield of Egypt, the guardian of its eastern door; it is the military bridge over which powerful Egypt crossed when it sought to rule the East, and conversely provided passage to the invading armies of the Hyksos, Assyrians, Persians, Greeks and Romans; later, the Arabs, Crusaders, Ottomans, French, English and others traveled this route seeking to conquer or dominate Egypt.

Sinai is a vast field of dramatic events. The area represents human life, continuously unfolding, and spiritual sentiments that also give it a celestial aura. It is the prophets' land, the peninsula of biblical Exodus, the place of the revelations of Moses, the birth place of monotheism, the land of the Old and New Testaments and of the Koran.

Sinai is also the land of hermitages, monasteries and churches; the area to which thousands of ancient Egyptian Christians fled from the discrimination and terror of their Roman occupiers; it is the sacred route of Christian journeys to Jerusalem and Moslem pilgrimages to Mecca.

Sinai was once a major trade route and a land rich in precious stones, metals and minerals, where thousands of Egyptians and Asians came in search of turquoise and copper.

Finally, Sinai today still attracts travelers, scientists, archeologists, businessmen, tourists, land reformers and, as in the past, mineral researchers and the military too.

Sinai: The Name

From this broad canvas, it might be assumed that the roots of the name *Sinai* might be easily derived, but that is not so. Despite the many stelae and inscriptions found in Sinai, and the role the peninsula played in Pharaonic history, we have not, until now, been able to ascertain a definite, consistent name that the ancient Egyptians gave to Sinai.

One of the names that referred to it was directly related to the ancient Egyptian word *mfkat*, which means turquoise. Sinai was also named in the inscriptions at

Opposite page:
El-Nawamis, a prehistoric religious site near Nuweiba.

the turquoise mines of Maghara in southwestern Sinai as "terraces of turquoise." In the list found at Luxor of foreign products used in the great temple, there was turquoise that came from Sinai, "the mountain of turquoise." The so-called Harris Papyrus dating to the 20th Dynasty (1188-1069 B.C.) refers to Sinai as the "Country of Turquoise."

The land of *Shsmt*, meaning malachite, may have been an early name referring to Sinai, which occurred in the Pyramid Texts found in some pyramids. The god Sopd was titled in the mines of Serabit El Khadem (also in southwestern Sinai) as "the Lord of Malachite." The land of Bia, or mines, which appeared in the inscriptions found at both of the main mine areas of the peninsula, may have meant *Sinai*.

The ancient inhabitants of Sinai practiced moon-cult rituals, a matter that was recorded in both Semitic and Greek sources. These suggest that the later name *Sinai* is derived from the name of Sin, the Semitic moon god, who might have been related to Thot, the Egyptian moon god, who was also venerated in Sinai.

The nomads of Sinai and their Asiatic neighbors were mentioned in the ancient Egyptian language variously as *Iabtyw* (the Easterners), *Hryw-Sha* (the sand dwellers), *Styw* (the arrow people), *Amw* (the nomad men), *Iwntyw* and *Imntyw* (the tribesmen) and *Shasw* (the Bedouin).

But over the millennia, all those names have vanished and been forgotten, while the name *Sinai*, which was used in the Old and New Testaments and in the Koran, is the only name that has survived and will continue to survive.

Sinai in Prehistoric Times

Beginning in the earliest prehistoric times (accounting for 95 percent of man's existence), Sinai was invaded by nomadic flint workers who came mostly from neighboring Asiatic regions on their way to Egypt. Paleolithic (Old Stone Age), Mesolithic (Middle Stone Age), Neolithic (New Stone Age) and Calaeolithic (Stone-Bronze Age) settlements have been found in various places, especially in Wadi El-Arish (northern Sinai), Tieh Plateau (middle Sinai) and Maghara, Serabit El Khadem and Wadi Serbal (in the south).

The stone and bronze tools, implements, weapons, pottery and vessels that were locally manufactured show a distinct resemblance to those discovered in Egypt, indicating that they were related to Egyptian culture. Occasionally these implements were more associated with those of southern Palestine, although there is no hard evidence of close connections between Egypt and Canaan through Sinai that long ago. At the same time, it is clear that in a land of transients like Sinai, immigrants may have settled and spread their cultural practices among the original inhabitants.

Archeological excavations show that dealings in turquoise and copper from Sinai occurred during Neolithic times and during Egyptian predynastic and protodynastic periods. Although this intercourse was on a limited scale in the beginning, it gradually increased. The relationship between the southern Sinai and the protodynastic culture of Naqgade in Egypt became stronger and more intense. Although some predynastic and protodynastic sites containing flint tools, pottery, bones and other finds were recently uncovered in northern Sinai, prehistoric research in the whole peninsula is still very limited. Sinai needs a wide and thorough survey followed by intense and continuous archeological excavations.

Sinai in Pharaonic Times

Egypt more or less dominated Sinai throughout its long Pharaonic history, which lasted about 3,000 years, from 3150 B.C. to 332 B.C. However, at the same time, the ancient Egyptians displayed little interest in Sinai except for mining in the South and strategic, military and defense needs in the North. Today, scholars are interested in Sinai mainly for its rock inscriptions dating to the Pharaonic period and for studying the route of the Exodus, which is believed to have occurred during the New Kingdom (1552-1069 B.C.).

Mining in Sinai

Although the ancient Egyptians did not exploit Sinai mines on a large scale, archeological evidence shows that they mined turquoise and copper in southern Sinai from the earliest times with a considerable amount of activity.

The British archeologist Francis Lewellyn Griffith was the first to begin a kind of survey and minor excavations in Sinai. But systematic archeology did not start there until the beginning of the 20th century. Another famous English archeologist Sir Flinders Petrie began the first scientific excavations in Maghara and Serabit El Khadem in 1904, and he published his findings in his great book *Researches in Sinai* in 1906.

But work in the mines of Maghara was revived by a British company in 1897, and many of the stelae and inscriptions were destroyed in its efforts to mine turquoise. It criminally blew up the old galleries to increase output, regardless of the fact that a piece of world heritage was lost. And the destruction was continued by the native inhabitants. Sir Petrie brought to the Egyptian Museum in Cairo most of what remained of those stelae and inscriptions. After Petrie, many scholars followed, such as the French archeologists Weil and Cledet, the Egyptian Mohamed Sheban, and more British – first Gardiner and then Cherny. Their work resulted in the discovery of an Egyptian temple, rock stelae, drawings and inscriptions.

All those finds leave no doubt about the purpose of the Pharaonic expeditions to Sinai: the description of the mining district of Maghara as the "Land of Turquoise" or the "terraces" or "mountain of turquoise" and naming Hathor, the goddess of the place, as "Mistress of Turquoise" surely indicates the intent of the ancient Egyptian expeditions. Another inscription discovered there mentions that copper deposits were found, too.

The Egyptian expeditions, making their way to southern Sinai, used one of two possible routes. One was the direct land route, and the other combined a crossing of the Suez Gulf or the Red Sea and then a land route leading to the mines. Inscriptions inform us that sometimes as many as 500 or more donkeys were used by the expeditions. Pharaonic mining expeditions were well equipped and supplied with the necessary food, and their camps were usually constructed beside the mines. Other Old Kingdom inscriptions (3rd to 6th dynasties) mention titles such as "crew recruits" or "overseer of ships" or "crews and ferrymen." That obviously means that there was water that had to be crossed at some point. Some inscriptions from the time of Amenemhat III, which the University of California expedition discovered in 1948, indicate the presence of an ancient harbor on the eastern coast of the Gulf of Suez south of Abu Zenema.

Maghara Mines

The earliest metallurgic working expeditions of the Old Kingdom

Following pages:
In North Sinai, waves of sand form high dunes, like this one near El-Arish.

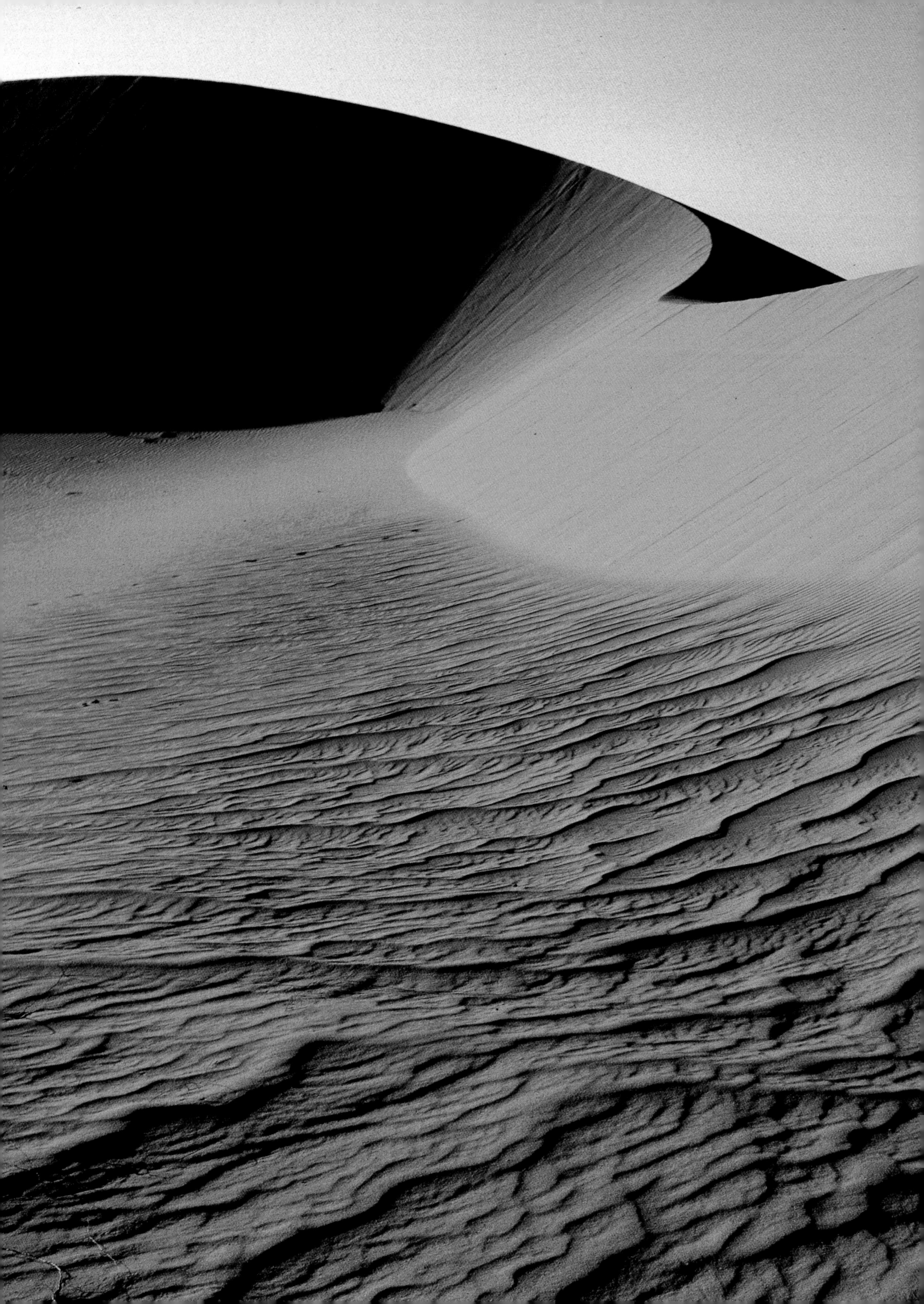

Above:
Rock with a proto-Synatic inscription, from Maghara. The alphabet of the inscription, deduced from hieroglyphics, is considered one of the earliest known.

Opposite page:
Rock relief depicts King Neu-Woser Re (5th Dynasty) smiting an enemy. It was found in Maghara.
Egyptian Museum, Cairo

were in Maghara, which means "the cave," a name that was given by the natives of Sinai to the inside of the mountain cliffs where the turquoise was found. On the eastern side of the cliffs are the remains of stone miners' rough huts, while on the western side are the entrances of the old mines and the places where rock inscriptions and stelae of the expeditions were found. Many of these were destroyed over the years; those that were saved were sent to the Egyptian Museum in Cairo. In Maghara, the Egyptians mined the greatest part of their turquoise supply, and it is evidence that turquoise represented the earliest contact between Egypt and Sinai.

The inscriptions of Maghara were carved on the rocks and recorded the glory of the Pharaonic kings. They show that the Egyptian expeditions covered the whole of the Old Kingdom (2700-2190 B.C.) and the 12th Dynasty (1991-1785 B.C.). The 6th Dynasty was represented by tablets of three kings, Djoser, Sekhem-Khet and Sanakht. The three succeeding dynasties show a series of tablets and inscriptions, especially those from the time of Senefru (4th Dynasty), Sahure and Neu-Woser Re (5th Dynasty).

The only rock tablet that was left in Maghara is that of King Sekhem-Khet that was formerly thought to be of King Semer-Khet from the 1st Dynasty (2950-2800 B.C.). It was engraved in deep relief on the smooth, natural surface of the cliff, about 400 feet above sea level. It shows three representations of the king. The first figure represents him with the red crown of Lower Egypt, and the second with the white crown of Upper Egypt. The third shows him in an elegant pose smiting an enemy with his mace. Above is the king's name placed inside a frame representing the facade of the palace, on which stands the god Horus in the form of a hawk. The whole sculptural work is excellent, with its free and smooth movements. What looks strange is that the scene was inscribed five feet higher from the ground than the surface of the spot, which makes it difficult to see from below.

An interesting rock carving that was brought from Maghara to the Egyptian Museum in Cairo is from the time of Senefru, founder of the 4th Dynasty. He was considered the dominator of Sinai and was deified there during the Middle Kingdom (covering a part of the 11th and all of the 12th dynasties, 2040-1785 B.C.). He ranked as one of its main gods along with Hathor, "Mistress of Turquoise," Sopd, "Lord of the East," and Thot. The scene was finely carved on red sandstone, depicting the names and epithets of the king in well-formed hieroglyphic signs. It depicts Senefru in a typical ancient Egyptian pose smiting an enemy.

The sculpture in red stone of King Neu-Woser Re (5th Dynasty), now also at the Egyptian Museum, is one of the largest brought from Maghara. It also represents the king smiting an enemy.

There follows a complete break with no trace of activity corresponding to the First Intermediate Period (7th-11th dynasties, 2200-2040 B.C.), and the royal names completely disappeared from Maghara. Apparently the internal disorder and weakness in Egypt proper ended any chance to send mining expeditions to Sinai.

Activity returned to Maghara during the Middle Kingdom and the old mines were reopened by King Mentuh Hotep II, the first king of the Middle Kingdom (11th Dynasty, 2040-2009 B.C.). He left many inscriptions identifying his activity during that period when Egyptian patronage of Sinai greatly increased. Thus, the Egyptians no longer depicted

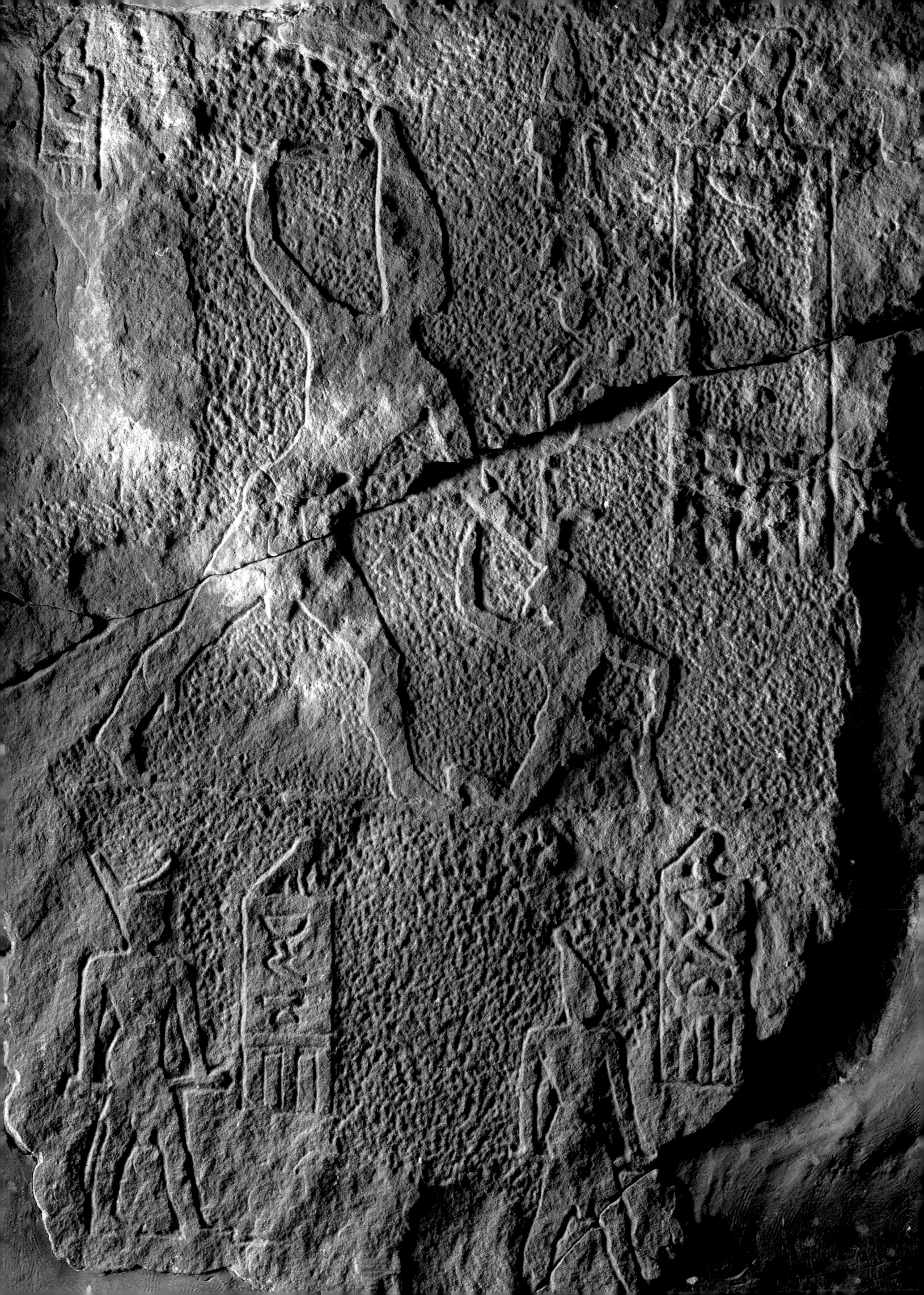

scenes of the king smiting Bedouin or Asians. The active and reformer kings of the 12th Dynasty reopened the routes to the mines of Sinai, but at the same time they began to shift from Maghara to Serabit El Khadem where copper mining took precedence over the traditional turquoise.

The Second Intermediate Period (13th-17th dynasties, 1785-1552 B.C.) showed another complete break similar to that of the First Intermediate Period, again because of great internal problems, especially those caused by the Hyksos occupation. The only inscription from the New Kingdom that escaped destruction was one dated the 16th year of the reign of Hatshepsut (18th Dynasty).

It is evident from inscriptions at Maghara that the prince of the *Rtnw* (Syrians), together with small groups of the *Amw* (nomad people) actively cooperated with the Egyptians in the mining. At the same time, some Asians were depicted armed with their own weapons, which suggests that they escorted miners to guard them against the attacks of both the Bedouin of Sinai and the other troublesome Asians, possibly because of the lack of Egyptian military forces.

Nowadays, reaching Maghara has become easier and more comfortable than in the past – through the Sidr Valley and Ikna Valley in southwestern Sinai. But, unfortunately, little can be seen there, since nearly all the Pharaonic inscriptions and stelae were either destroyed by the British mining company or the natives mentioned earlier, or transferred to the Egyptian Museum in Cairo 90 years ago. But the visitor is compensated by the magnificence of nature. Lofty mountains and sloping valleys change by the minute with the shifting clouds; and through a visit and reflection upon the silent, ancient settlements, one can sense the lives and struggles of the miners who once crowded the area no less than 5,000 years ago.

Serabit El Khadem Mines

Serabit El Khadem (whose meaning is uncertain) is located a little to the northwest of Maghara on a high plateau atop a mountain. It is defined by curving valleys, whose geological structure is the same as that in Maghara. The main group of mines were worked for both turquoise and copper. Stone tools used by the ancient miners were found in the area, and some, made of copper, were fashioned into chisels, crushers, scrapers, mallets and axes.

Despite the loss of a large number of inscriptions, which deteriorated or were destroyed or stolen, hundreds more were found in Serabit. No evidence was found to indicate that the Egyptians had mined the site earlier than the beginning of the 12th Dynasty (1991-1785 B.C.) – the same time that the Maghara mines were deserted.

The earliest carvings date to the reign of Sesostris II in the 12th Dynasty (1895-1878 B.C.). Serabit inscriptions can be divided into three main categories. The first is composed mainly of the royal inscriptions that were depicted near the entrances to the mines, and these did not include any significant relief. The second category is composed of inscriptions and reliefs depicted on the surfaces of the walls of the Temple of Hathor at Serabit that dated to the Middle Kingdom. These mentioned names and epithets of various kings who participated in building the temple or in decorating it, and they easily reveal the full history of the temple. The third category comprises inscriptions depicted on free-standing stelae, commemorating the various mining expeditions that came to the site. All those inscriptions belong to the Middle and New kingdoms. There are no inscriptions from the Late Period (21st-30th dynasties, 1069-332 B.C.), during which the Sinai mines were abandoned. The Egyptians then became more dependent on the mines of the Eastern Desert and their main interest in the peninsula was the Way of Horus, the famous military route in northern Sinai.

Some small objects found inside the temple or near the mines, such as figurines, bracelets, rings, tablets and stone vases, were also inscribed. An excellent small portrait of Queen Tye, wife of Amenophis III (18th Dynasty), which was carved on a green stone, was discovered by Petrie in 1904. It belonged to a statue surely dedicated to this Temple of Hathor. Although it is not more than seven centimeters high, it clearly represents a noble and determined woman who was still in her youth.

The Temple of Hathor was initially built during the 12th Dynasty and later was reconstructed several times. Its remains are located at the end of the plateau. This temple was the sole place of worship in Sinai. No doubt its main aim was to protect the mines, to assure the success of their production, and to give sacred dignity to the place. Its main goddess, Hathor, might have been the equivalent of a local goddess that Petrie has associated with the Semitic goddess Ishtar. The god next in importance to Hathor in the temple and whose sanctuary lay beside it was the god Sopd, who was identified with Horus and sometimes was depicted as a crouching hawk beside his other representation in human forms.

Some scholars think that the temple was used for Semitic religious practices and sacrifices by the Bedouin tribes. They cite as evidence quantities of timber ashes resulting from Semitic burnt sacrifices, the discovery of two dedicated conic stones in the temple, and the remains of basins and tanks that might have been used in ablution ceremonies.

The opposing view is that burnt sacrifices were also known in Egypt, and the conic stones may have been grinding stones used by the miners, while the basins and tanks could have been used for water purification, which also played a role in Egyptian rituals. So, most probably, the ceremonial rituals practiced in the Temple of Serabit El Khadem did not differ much from those practiced in Egypt, and the worship of Egyptian gods in Sinai such as Hathor and Sopd was similar to practices followed in Egypt.

At the same time, it is plausible that Semitics who were not slaves or prisoners worked with the Egyptians in Serabit, and may have been permitted to perform their Semitic rituals in the temple, alongside the Egyptian rituals.

Finally it must be stated that the mining area, especially around the temple at Serabit, needs extensive archeological work. It will require a master plan based on surveys, clearance, digging and research for the missing blocks and monuments that belonged to the temple or were related to the site. It also needs full documentation, restoration, preservation and protection against human and natural elements that threaten the site. The site should also be prepared to facilitate the visit of tourists and others.

Other Metallurgic Centers

Archeological evidence at other mining areas in Sinai indicate that during the Middle Kingdom activity shifted, as at Serabit El Khadem, to mining copper.
The last great copper-mining king

Above:
Sculpted head of Queen Tye, mother of Akhenaton, uncovered at Serabit El Khadem in 1904.
h. 7 cm.
Egyptian Museum, Cairo.

Following pages:
Inscribed stelae stand among the ruins of the Temple of Hathor at Serabit El Khadem. Inscriptions commemorate the mining expeditions that came to exploit the rich veins of turquoise and copper.

was Ramses III (20th Dynasty, 1186-1154 B.C.).

Inscriptions testify that Wadi Nasib, which was not far from Serabit, was a copper-mining and smelting center. A stele found there, dating to the time of Amenemhat III in the 12th Dynasty, proves that there was active mining in the area since the Middle Kingdom. Wadi Kharit, directly to the west of Serabit, had a similar activity dating from the Middle Kingdom, according to the rock inscriptions. This supports the idea that the work in both mining sites followed the mining period of Serabit El Khadem.

Other areas, such as Wadi Um Thamians and Wadi Roud El Eer (both near Maghara) also show traces of copper mining. All this is evidence of the economic importance of mining in the Sinai.

Strategic and Military Importance of Sinai

During the Archaic Period (1st-2nd dynasties, 2950-2675 B.C.) and the Old Kingdom, Sinai was considered a hostile area, and the Egyptians regarded its people as beneath the level of civilization. During those periods, the early Egyptian kings successively struggled with the inhabitants of Sinai and tried to subjugate them, and it seems that the better-armed Egyptian troops succeeded.

But when Egypt almost fell apart during the First Intermediate Period (7th-11th dynasties, 2190-2040 B.C.), a large number of Asian nomads from Palestine infiltrated the Nile Delta and remained, destroying aspects of civilization there. The Egyptians succeeded in driving them out only with the rise of the Middle Kingdom (11th-12th dynasties, 2046-1674 B.C.).

Egypt seemed to attain some sort of peaceful relationship with the Sinai's inhabitants and the neighboring Palestinian Bedouin during the Middle Kingdom, as indicated by the collaboration of those groups in the mining operations there. Later, during the Second Intermediate Period (13th-17th dynasties, 1756-1550 B.C.) the Hyksos tribes moved across Sinai towards a weak and divided Egypt and occupied most of the country. Later still, Egypt's struggle for independence compelled the Hyksos to retreat back through Sinai to the fortified Sharuhin in the Gaza Strip, where they were finally defeated by Ahmose I. During the New Kingdom (18th-20th dynasties, 1550-1526 B.C.) a strong Egypt used northern Sinai as a route for its triumphant armies to defeat enemies in Palestine, Syria and Lebanon; while during the Late Period, Egypt scarcely used Sinai as a means or route to defeat Palestine and Syria. On the contrary Egypt was defeated by ambitious conquerors such as the Assyrian Assurbanipal, the Persian Cambyses and the Macedonian Alexander the Great. All used Sinai for their military purposes.

The Way of Horus

Most of the routes through Sinai in Pharaonic times were mainly caravan routes and desert tracks, some of which might have been in use since prehistoric times. But, during the New Kingdom, the coastal strip of northern Sinai became the main land bridge over which the military operations and commerce passed between Africa and Asia, and especially between the Eastern Nile Delta and Canaan. The main and most important route, which ran not far from Sinai's Mediterranean coast, was named in the ancient Egyptian sources as "the Way of Horus" (an epithet of the king). This can be considered the world's most ancient and significant military route and was used by both the Egyptians as conquerors and the conquerors of Egypt.

Evidence shows that the Egyptians secured this vital route by providing it with a chain of forts, stations and water supplies (wells, tanks, basins, etc).

The forts were constructed not only to facilitate the movement of Egyptian troops, but also to control communications and secure trade operations. Each fort was usually named after the Pharaoh who built it.

Historical records give testament to the military fitness and efficiency of the Way of Horus. Inscriptions at Karnak mention that the armies of Thutmose III marched from Seila (Tharou) to Gaza, in the East, crossing North Sinai, a distance of about 150 miles, in just ten days.

No significant finds or important remains along the Way of Horus were discovered until recently. That undoubtedly is a result of the battles fought along many sections of the route over thousands of years, which surely ruined the sites. Other reasons are the pillage of the ancient settlements by the Bedouin who lived around the route as well as deterioration caused by sandstorms and other natural elements. Finally, unfortunately, archeological excavations, surveys and wide investigations have not yet been carried out and are greatly needed in that area.

Historical records also show that major renewals of the fortifications and stations along the Way of Horus were celebrated by reliefs carved on the exterior northern wall of the great hypostyle hall built in the Temple of Amon at Karnak following the new development and renovation of the Egyptian military by Seti I (19th Dynasty, 1294-1270 B.C.). In addition, the Anstasi Papyrus, assigned to the reign of Ramses II (son of Seti I) listed in geographical order the fortified stations along that military route. It also listed some cities in northern Canaan, as there was notable interest in that neighboring land during Egypt's New Kingdom Period. Those two Egyptian records attest to the strategic importance of this route during the New Kingdom, although this route was mentioned in earlier documents, as for example, in the well-known Sinuhi Story (early 12th Dynasty), which mentioned Sinuhi's return to Egypt via this northern Sinai route after his long stay in Palestine.

Today, only a few of the approximately 20 stations and forts along the route can be recognized. Gaza, for example, is "the city of Canaan" referred to, and Raphia is now known as Rafah in the east, and Tharou to the west. Tharou, a Greek settlement now known as Tel Siefa (about two miles to the east of the Kantara Sharqi), was probably the most important fortification in western Sinai. Migdol was one of the largest settlements and its remains are about one mile from the modern town of Tel El Heer. It is considered a fortified defensive citadel, and recently, a Roman camp and kiln were discovered there. Other posts cannot today be identified for certain, since they mostly took the names and titles of the two military kings, Seti I and Ramses II (the Great), who led the Egyptian armies in the invasion of Palestine and Syria and returned triumphantly to Egypt using the Way of Horus.

For more than 200 years, from 1154 to 945 B.C., there were no important military expeditions through the Way of Horus either out of Egypt or into Egypt from Asia. But, later, Schechonq (called Shishak in the Old Testament), the founder of the Libyan dynasty called the 22nd (945-715 B.C.), launched his armies, and used the famous route to invade Jerusalem and capture the treasures of the Temple of

Following pages:
From its strategic position on an island in the Gulf of Aqaba, the 12th-century Citadel of Saladin defended pilgrims and caravans against Christian Crusaders.

Solomon. The Assyrians also used the same route to invade Egypt during the first half of the 6th century B.C.

Neckao II (610-595 B.C.), the second Pharaoh of the Asiatic period (22nd Dynasty), led his army with Greek mercenaries to northern Sinai in 625 B.C. to invade Palestine and Syria. But he was badly defeated by the Babylonian King Napopolosser in 605 B.C. in the battle of Carkemish in northern Syria. This was the last Egyptian military expedition sent by the Pharaohs to western Asia through Sinai. At the same time, archeological evidence shows that Greek mercenaries and merchants settled during that period on the western edge of Sinai.

Some years later, the Persians used the Way of Horus to invade Egypt twice. The first conquest was led by Cambyses (who established the 27th Dynasty) in 525 B.C. Herodotus tells us that the native inhabitants of Sinai helped Cambyses in his passage through northern Sinai, an assertion for which evidence has not yet been found.

The second Persian invasion of Egypt was at the end of the 30th Dynasty (380-332 B.C.). The Persians remained for only a few years before they were expelled by Alexander the Great in 332 B.C. This terminated the Pharaonic period, and Egypt entered a new, long phase of its history, the Graeco-Roman period.

Proto-Synatic Inscriptions

Among the cultural achievements related to Sinai is the earliest alphabetic script invented, the so-called Proto-Synatic or Synatic inscriptions. These were found carved on the rocks at Maghara, Serabit El Khadem and Wadi Nasib. Scholars date them to the New Kingdom or perhaps even as early as the Middle Kingdom. The script was used by the miners during their work and habitation there. Some scholars state that this script was derived from hieroglyphics, and that it was the basis from which the Phoenicians invented their alphabet, which, in turn, is the mother of the modern Western alphabet. Hopefully, archeologists will eventually shed some light on the steps that originally led to the formation of this script, its place in time, and other details.

Graeco-Roman and Byzantine Period

In 332 B.C., Egypt was easily invaded and occupied – with the help of the Egyptian populace – by Alexander the Great of Macedonia. After his death in 323 B.C., Alexander's successors, the Ptolemies, set up a Hellenistic kingdom that ruled the country from a new capital, Alexandria, for about 300 years until Cleopatra VII and her ally Antonius were defeated in the battle of Actium just before her dramatic death. Egypt then became just another province in the vast Roman Empire.

In A.D. 395, after the decline and division of the Roman Empire, Egypt became a part of the Christian Byzantine Empire, whose Christian philosophy and theories differed from those adopted by the Copts (Egyptian Christians). The Coptic Church became the center of national resistance to Constantinople's Byzantine Empire, which discriminated badly against the Egyptians. Later, in 640, the Arab General Amr Ibn El-As crossed Sinai and invaded Egypt, which became an Islamic province under the Caliphate domain.

Classical historians and geographers – Greeks and Romans such as Herodotus, Strabo, Ptolemy and Josephus – showed a notable interest in Sinai because of its strategic, political, and religious importance, although their information was limited in many important aspects, such as those concerning cultural background, settlements and economic resources. Maps such as the Table of Peutinger and the Antonine Itinerary of the Byzantine period did not neglect Sinai or its routes.

Sinai was the main field of battles between the Ptolemies and their rivals, the rulers of Syria. One of the decisive battles was that of Rafah (Raphia) in 217 B.C. between Ptolemy IV Philopator and Antiochus IV, king of Syria. The battle ended with the victory of Ptolemy IV because Egyptian native soldiers fought alongside his forces.

In Pelusium (today called Tell El Farma) in western Sinai, Pompey was killed by the men of Ptolemy XII (80-51 B.C.), in spite of Ptolemy's promise to protect him against Caesar. The Emperor Hadrian (A.D. 117-138) passed Pelusium as he returned from Syria and ordered a temple of Zeus to be built on the site to commemorate Pompey's death there. Nearby, the ruins of a Roman fort, fortifications, a theater and a bridge, as well as those of a Byzantine church and an Islamic mosque indicate the importance of this site over successive periods.

At the same time, Sinai's sandy and rocky soil discouraged planting and agriculture, and the Romans were not interested in mining turquoise or copper or other similar activities. Consequently, the Romans considered Sinai, especially its coastal area, as essential only to their communications system and to trade between the East and West. Of course they also valued its military and strategic importance.

Because of Rome's oppression and discrimination against the pious Egyptian Christians, many of them fled to remote parts of Egypt's deserts, especially to Sinai, where they secretly built monasteries, hermitages and churches, preferring, of course, to be as near as possible to Moses' places of revelation. But starting late in the 4th century, after the conversion of the Romans to the new religion, and after Theodosus' edict that proclaimed Christianity in 389 as the only religion throughout the empire, churches and monasteries were built everywhere. Pilgrimages that crossed northern Sinai to Jerusalem or southern Sinai to the Mountain of Moses, or Mount Sinai, became frequent.

A major route to Palestine was developed that followed the direction of the northern coast of Sinai, but was a short distance inland. It is thought that this was the route taken by the Holy Family as they fled into Egypt. Because Christians visited the places of revelation, many inscriptions were inscribed on the rocks, especially on the surface of the valleys.

Besides the ruins of Roman fortresses, churches and settlements from the 4th century A.D., many coins, pieces of pottery, mosaics and artifacts from everyday life were found in northern Sinai sites such as Flossiat (Philasia), Beir El Abd, Mohamadia (Gerrum), Tel El Heer, Tell El Habbou, Plusine and Rafah. (The latter's classical name was Rhinocorura, which means "those with broken noses." The ancient Egyptians used to punish criminals by breaking their noses and then sending the offending individuals to remote places.) In the southern Sinai, ruins of a settlement were found in Wadi Firan, while a fort at Dahab was recently unearthed.

In many Sinai valleys, beside the Greek and Latin inscriptions, a huge number of Nabatean inscriptions were found, especially in Wadi Maktoub (which means

Opposite page:
Arab inscription found at El Naqab in the central region of Sinai dates from the time of Abdul-Nasr Konswa El-Ghory, one of the 16th-century Mamluk sultans who were responsible for safeguarding the trading route between East and West that criss-crossed Sinai.

"valley of inscriptions"). This is about four miles from Maghara. Those inscriptions may not be considered as historical sources by some scholars since most of them are composed of only a word or a short sentence. But at the same time, they have a value for linguistic, epigraphic and documentation studies.

The Nabataens were Arab tribes that had been Hellenized. Although they established a kingdom that covered what is now southern Jordan and extended northwest to what today is Saudi Arabia, they often wandered in neighboring Sinai and carried out trade activities. The Nabataens continued to exist in the peninsula even after their subjugation by the Romans and later through the Byzantine period.

The Islamic Period

In A.D. 640, two years after Jerusalem fell into the hands of the Arabs, Amir El Momeneen (whose title was Prince of Believers or Caliph) Omar Ibn El Khatab, gave permission to his Moslem troops to conquer Egypt. So, 4,000 soldiers headed by General Amr Ibn El-As advanced towards the Nile Delta and Valley, along Sinai's northern coastal route starting from Gaza and arriving at Pelusium (Tell El Farma). The Egyptians were not prepared to fight or resist since the Byzantines had badly discriminated against them for their religious differences, and the Arabs easily dominated the whole of Egypt including Sinai, which was placed under the rule of Omayed Caliphs in Damascus. A few years later, the Arab leader Abdulla Iban El Serh crossed Sinai with his army to reach Egypt's new Islamic capital, "El Fustat," established in A.D. 642, north of Old Cairo; from there he moved westward to invade North Africa and convert its people to the new faith: Islam. Egypt then became an Islamic country, most of its inhabitants were converted to Islam, and the Arabic language replaced Coptic.

During the Roman and Byzantine eras, the trade caravan routes were controlled by the successive ruling authorities. But this control shifted into the hands of Sinai's nomadic tribes under the new Arab rulers, who considered those routes as mere transit ways in a no-man's-land. After a time, those rulers became concerned about Sinai and started to look after the order and discipline needed there.

The first reason was strategic and military: the immutable fact that Sinai was always (and still is) the main civil and military gateway to Egypt. Countless armies marched eastward whenever an Egyptian ruler felt capable of defeating his Asian enemies or extending Egypt's territory abroad. On the other hand, countless foreign rulers tried – and sometimes succeeded – in marching through Sinai to conquer Egypt. The second reason was the fact that the best way to protect Egypt from its invaders was to try to fight them before they even reached Sinai.

Islamic Egypt's rulers repeatedly sent armies across Sinai. Thus, Sinai was used as a military route again during the time of the Caliphates, from 641 until 1914 and the Ottoman occupation.

In the midst of that period, about the 12th century, the Crusaders moved from Palestine and Syria through northern Sinai to conquer Egypt. The name of Lake Berdawil, that large body of water on the Mediterranean in northern Sinai, got its name from King Berdawil, who ruled Jerusalem for a short time and who was killed near the lake in 1117 during his attempt to invade Egypt.

During this period Egypt's rulers were responsible for protecting Moslem pilgrims from Egypt,

northern Africa and even the Sahara who crossed Sinai on their journeys to Mecca. Around 875, Ahmed Ibn Toulon, the founder of the Toulunide dynasty, tried to improve the pilgrimage route by supplying it with water pools and reservoirs, digging wells and providing some other accommodations.

Egypt's rulers during the Islamic period, especially during the Mamluk reign, were also guardians of trade between the East and West, as well as of shipping in the Gulf of Aqaba.

All these facts explain why forts, fortifications and citadels throughout Sinai – some dating from the Pharaonic and Graeco-Roman periods – were continuously being repaired, renewed and resecured. As mentioned earlier, most of them are now in ruins because of later wars and the elements.

The citadel that is in considerably better condition than the others in Sinai, and apparently was a large and important one, is that of Saladin on the island of Pharoon (a name most probably derived from the Latin word *phara*, which means lighthouse). It displays historical, architectural and strategic values that are unique compared to other Islamic monuments of the peninsula. It was a marine base, a guardian that foretold any threat of danger and a defender of the area surrounding it, especially during the conflict with the Crusaders.

Its location was highly favorable: It was not far from other important posts – about 8 kilometers from Taba and 60 kilometers from Nuweiba; it is about 250 meters from the shore, and it could easily be supplied through land routes with food, water, and ammunition – all the items a soldier needed to live and fight.

Although Pharoon Island was used militarily in earlier Islamic times before Saladin, and might even have been used in Byzantine times, it is certain that the present citadel was designed and constructed by Saladin about 1170. It continued to safeguard pilgrims and the caravan routes in time of peace as well as war.

The citadel was actually composed of independent forts facing each other on two hills. Between them stood a mosque. The citadel was enclosed by an outer wall, and its towers overlooked the Gulf of Aqaba, the caravan routes and the vast surrounding area. It is a monument to architectural planning and harmony with its natural setting.

The citadel has been seriously damaged by wars, climatic conditions and lack of conservation. A great deal of archeological work must be undertaken to clean, excavate, restore and preserve it. It is nearly the only surviving example of its kind, and it is of great value historically, architecturally and archeologically.

The remains of another citadel built by Saladin stand at the entrance to Wadi Sidr. It is the Gindi Citadel, which was used to ward off attacks by the Crusaders. It had a surrounding wall, a great mosque and a gate that was decorated with Arabic inscriptions. Its plan seems to have been similar to that of the citadel on Pharoon Island.

The fortress of Nakhl was constructed on the pilgrimage route, named Darb El Hajj (the Hajj way), that crossed the Tieh Plateau. It is located 180 miles from Suez, and 70 miles from Aqaba. The pilgrimage route was not built until well into Egypt's Islamic period, so the fort of Nakhl was probably constructed to protect the pilgrimage route and as a supply post for pilgrims en route to Mecca.

Only a very few parts of other fortresses survive. Those include Arish, Nuweiba, Tina, Balah, Akba and El-Tor, where a Japanese archeological team has been excavating. They recently succeeded in unearthing the remains of some buildings believed to date back to the Ottoman era.

The ambitious El Salam (Peace) Canal project in northern Sinai, which Egypt began to dig in 1991, threatens both archeological sites where excavation is underway and those still buried, all along the canal and in the cultivatable lands around it. Thus, Egypt recently began an international campaign to unearth Sinai's cultural heritage through intensive excavations in the threatened area. The government's Organization of Egyptian Antiquities has requested help at scores of sites that are endangered by the digging of the canal, its water distribution and its drains, as well as by the planned agricultural development and urbanization of hundreds of thousands of acres. The appeal also covers a project that will widen the Suez Canal along its eastern shore, and which threatens archeological sites near there as well.

Fortunately, response to the appeal has been great, and hundreds of Egyptian and foreign missions are excavating in the threatened areas and have uncovered many interesting monuments and historical objects. It is hoped that this campaign will add valuable information to the story of the religious, political, cultural and military role of the Sinai Peninsula over Egypt's successive millennia.

Triangle of Grandeur

by Dr. Fouad Iskandar

Perhaps no other region in the world has been brought to the forefront of man's knowledge as rapidly as the Sinai has over the last four decades or so. No one can deny that this region of the Middle East has been a fulcrum about which much of the modern history of the Middle East turns, and thus much of the world's.

The Sinai Peninsula is described as the meeting place of Africa and Asia. It forms a triangle, with its base in the north abutting the Mediterranean Sea, and its apex in the south at a point where the Red Sea forms the southern boundary of the peninsula. Out of Egypt's total area of about one million square kilometers, the peninsula occupies about 61,000, or roughly six percent.

Sinai lies mainly between the two northern fingers of the Red Sea: the Gulf of Suez and the Gulf of Aqaba. The latter forms part of Africa's Great Rift Valley, which extends more than 6,000 kilometers from Mozambique north through the continent, into Palestine and the Dead Sea. The Sinai Peninsula sits isolated between the Gulf of Suez and the Suez Canal in the West, and the Gulf of Aqaba and the Negev Desert to the East.

The peninsula runs roughly 320 kilometers (130 miles) from east to west, and about 590 kilometers (240 miles) from north to south.

Sinai's geographical relief is of interesting origin. The peninsula occupies an ancient block, a portion of the African Precambrian Shield (more than 570 million years old) that rose between two rift areas and tilted down in a northerly direction. Between the Precambrian and the Quaternary Period (which began about 2.5 million years ago), it was subject to both long and short incursions of the Tethys Sea and, later, of the Mediterranean Sea. Sinai's desert is separated from Egypt's Eastern Desert by the Gulf of Suez and the Suez Canal, but continues eastward into the Negev Desert of Israel without marked change of relief.

Sinai can be divided into three principal physical regions.

The Al-Tor region comprises the southern complex of high mountains of igneous rock. Some of the highest peaks in Egypt are found in this region, such as Mount Catherine (2,642 meters high), Mount Om Shomer (2,585 meters), and Mount Sinai, or Jebal Musa (2,285 meters). This region is extremely rugged and sharply incised by a large number of deep, canyon-like valleys or seasonal watercourses. Such valleys or *wadis* are mostly dry and drain sharply toward the Gulf of Suez in the west or the Gulf of Aqaba in the east. This southern giant mountain mass is separated from the Gulf of Suez by a narrow coastal plain known as Al-Qaa, which is four to twelve kilometers wide. This western plain is much wider than the coastal plain that skirts the Gulf of Aqaba in the

Opposite page:
Phantasmagoric rock formations such as this one are found in the Al-Tih plateau of central Sinai. The region is formed mainly of limestone and rises 1,200 meters above sea level.

Following pages:
A singular acacia stands tall in the middle of the dry Wadi Khreza off the road to Dahab. Beyond the tree, a mangrove swamp edges into the Gulf of Aqaba.

east, where land rises precipitously from the gulf.

The second principal physical region is the Al-Tih tableland or plateau, which is the central region of the peninsula. The plateau is formed mainly of limestone and rises an average of 1,200 meters above sea level. It slopes northward to the region along the Mediterranean Sea. This rocky area has very few water wells and a thinner population than the rest of Sinai.

The third area is the northern region commonly referred to as the El-Arish plains. This region slopes from the highlands in the south, northward to the Mediterranean. It is characterized by the extensive plain of El-Arish, by dry valleys, and by northern coastal plains that are broken up by masses of hills and tracts of mostly fixed sand dunes. The region represents a main drainage basin in which El-Arish Valley acts as a master stream emptying into the Mediterranean near the town of El-Arish. This region is the most densely populated part of Sinai, although that is relative, of course. The population of El-Arish is about 50,000.

Added to the limitations created by the complex relief of the peninsula, is that imposed by the desert itself. Sinai falls within the great arid belt that crosses northern Africa and southwestern Asia. It is manifested in Sinai by a degraded soil surface, sand-dune expanses, salinization, and dry watercourses. In the North, the Mediterranean low region, the climate in winter is unstable, with relatively high rainfall (125 millimeters); in summer it is dry and intensely hot with hot sandy winds called *al-khamasin*. In the southern region, summer is hot and winter is cold due to the mountainous terrain. The prominent peaks are covered with clouds throughout the year, and some of them are covered with ice and snow in winter.

The Sinai region suffers great temperature extremes that vary by area and season. In the North, winter temperatures can range from 20 degrees Celsius to a low of 7 degrees Celsius (45°F); the summer maximum reaches 37 degrees Celsius (99°F), and the minimum 18 degrees Celsius. Meanwhile, in the South, the winter temperatures can range from 27 degrees Celsius (81°F) down to 13 degrees Celsius (55°F); summer temperatures mount to a high of 35 degrees Celsius (95°F), down to 25 degrees Celsius (77°F). Sinai's prevailing winds come mainly from the north. Severe wind storms occur in the north once every three years or so. Relative humidity is generally high on the coasts, reaching 74 percent along the Mediterranean and 60 percent along the two gulfs of the Red Sea. Foggy intervals vary from four to six days a month in northern Sinai to one to three days a month in central Sinai.

Sinai also has varied vegetation. In the south, where metamorphic and igneous rocks predominate, land is mainly barren, while scrub survives on the steep slopes as well as on the plateau to the north. In the central plateau and the northern plains, desert detritus occurs. These areas include stretches of alluvial soils in Wadi El-Arish and the dune complex of northwest Sinai. Succulents and salt-tolerant plants are found especially on the subdesert coastal plains. Medicinal and fodder plants are widely distributed. Occasional animals are ibex, gazelles, sand foxes, hares, hedgehogs and moles. Falcons and eagles are indigenous. There are also seasonal migrants such as quail, partridge and grouse.

The People of Sinai

If Sinai is thought of mainly as the land through which Moses led the Exodus from Egypt, history records that the peninsula witnessed many crossings in both directions. Rarely, however, have people settled there. Over the millennia, the rough relief and difficult physical conditions of the peninsula could not stop waves of invaders from pouring into the Nile Valley and Delta from the east; nor could these natural factors stop Egyptians from driving those invaders out of the country, across Sinai, and even to continue their march into the lands that lie to the east, northeast and southeast.

Thus, Sinai accommodates a scant population of about 225,000, or about half of one percent of Egypt's population. There is no doubt that its population distribution is a normal result of the peninsula's tough physical geography. More than 70 percent of the population is concentrated in the northern fringe of the peninsula, where water supplies are adequate, and in the western fringe, where petroleum and manganese industries have been developed. The other parts to the south, which are mainly high, rugged mountain areas are very sparsely settled. Yet, due to the limitations of the desert environment, less than 45 percent of the population are settled at all; the rest are Bedouin nomads who roam the region. The settled population engages in agriculture and land reclamation, and in petroleum mining and fishing. A much more recent activity has been tourism, an activity that will be examined in more detail later on.

The wandering Bedouin tribes migrate, seeking water and pasturage; few are attracted to industry or agriculture. There are southern and northern groups; the southern group, known as *Twara*, inhabits all Sinai south of Darb El Hajj; the principal tribes of this group are the *Eleigat* of northwest Sinai, the *Sawallha* of southwest Sinai, and the *Umm Zeina* of east Sinai, particularly along the Gulf of Aqaba. The northern group has no distinctive name and consists of a collection of tribes, which have mostly migrated from Arabia. It includes principally the *Tarabin*, the largest tribe in Sinai; the *Tiaha* of east-central Sinai; the *Hueitat* of west-central Sinai; and the *Aiada* and the *Eheiwat* of Northwest Sinai.

Strikingly different from the natives of Sinai, a community of Eastern Orthodox Christian monks lives in the Monastery of St. Catherine in the mountainous South (see chapter starting on page 73).

Humankind's existence in Sinai was, until two decades or so ago, very much at nature's sufferance. Geographical controls – notably those exerted by geology, relief and climate – restricted, even determined, where man could live and what he could do. The Egyptian-Israeli wars of 1956, 1967 and 1973 marked a new era for man in Sinai; he has been able to modify considerably the effect of natural conditions – and even turn them to his advantage.

One example is transportation and communications. In the early 1930s, Sinai's principal roads were desert tracks running from west to east. The northernmost of these was a track following the ancient Way of Horus, linking Al Qantara on the Suez Canal with Rafah on the Mediterranean coast. There were two central tracks – the Syrian track that ran between Ismailia on the Canal and Abu Uwagilad, and a track running from Suez to Al-Quasymah via Al-Hasana, a route in use since the 16th century B.C. The southernmost track was the most important in Sinai and was variously known as Darb El Hajj, or el-Darb as Sultany, dating from the 13th century B.C. It was the pilgrims' road running from Suez

The falcon (opposite page) *and the owl* (above) *are familiar inhabitants of North Sinai.*

Following pages:
Bedouin women with their children are on the move near Wadi Gharandal. A youngster urges a donkey to bring up the rear.

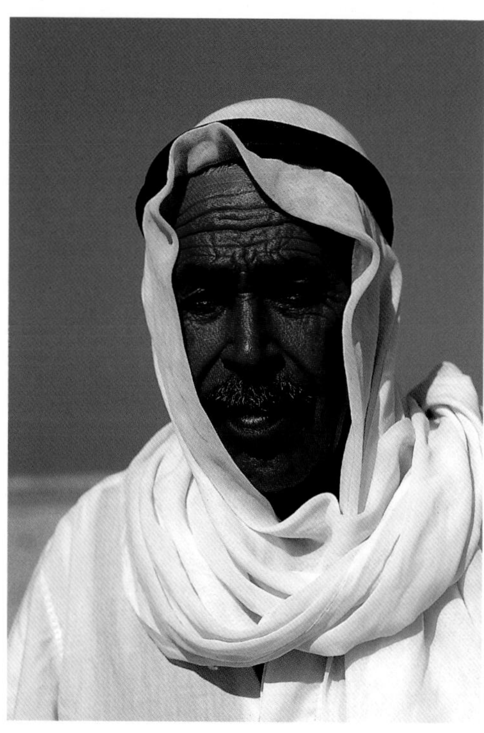

Above:
A Bedouin farmer from El-Arish wears the traditional Oqal, *or headdress. Forty percent of Egypt's cultivable land is located in Sinai. Numerous land reclamation projects are under way, including one to pump Nile water into the region through a culvert under the Suez Canal.*

to Aqaba via om-Nakhl.

After 1936, the peninsula's infrastructure was meant to serve military purposes. Paved roads and railway lines were constructed to that end, along with a number of military air bases. With the 1967 war, the shape of the road network changed completely and the railway line in the North was destroyed. Meanwhile, military purposes continued to dictate the shape of the network, along with the needs of the mining regions and the newly developed tourist centers, especially those looking on the Gulf of Aqaba and in the region of St. Catherine's Monastery. The 1973 war brought about a completely different picture. Today, paved roads in Sinai total more than 3,200 kilometers. In 1980, a modern telephone network was started up. By 1994, Sinai had six civil airports and several landing strips in scattered, economically important locations. Several harbors have been developed along the coastlines of both the Gulf of Suez and the Gulf of Aqaba. Changes like these have had a significant positive impact on human habitation in the peninsula.

In fact, most human practices in Sinai could be considered within ecological patterns evident in the peninsula. There is no doubt that these patterns have had great influence on the human and social life of the natives in the different regions of the peninsula. Although drastic changes are taking place in the social fabric of some Sinai communities, it is evident that these ecological patterns are so deep-rooted that they are likely to influence societal patterns for many years to come.

In the northern region, economic and social life are affected by dependence on fishing and agriculture, although the traditional nomadic pattern continues to exist in the region as well. Thus, it is clear that a variety of human behavioral patterns mix and intermingle in the region. In other words, a native may tend to show behavior that indicates he belongs to one specific pattern, yet practices other activities at the same time.

Along Sinai's Mediterranean coastline, a marine ecology prevails and economic and social life revolves principally around fishing. A fact worth mentioning here is that although Sinai represents only six percent of Egypt's total area, its coastline represents about 700 kilometers or about 29 percent of Egypt's total.

Lake Berdawil in northern Sinai is another determining ecological factor. It is joined to the Mediterranean by narrow straits that help regulate the flow of water and fish into and out of it. The lake has an area of about 165,000 *feddans*, or 70,000 acres, is more than 90 kilometers (54 miles) long, and its circumference exceeds 750 kilometers (450 miles). It is separated from the Mediterranean by a sandy strip, which is mostly less than one kilometer wide. About 15 to 20 percent of the population of northern Sinai depends on the lake for its livelihood. Four cooperatives operate in the lake, with 3,000 members who own about 950 fishing boats. Fishing is prohibited from December to April to allow fish to grow to an economic size. Since the 1960s, the lake has played an important economic role nationally. It contributes about 60 percent of total Egyptian fish exports and represents receipts of about US$15 million out of a total for the fishing industry of about $25.5 million.

The plains south of the Mediterranean coastal region are Sinai's most densely populated region, again a result of ecological factors. This region receives more rain, although rainfall is still relatively scarce. It is also a region that has a considerable wealth of underground water, which shows in the chain of springs and wells along the extension of fixed sand dunes. The region is crossed by the dry Valley of El-Arish, which is more than 230 kilometers long. The valley becomes a flowing river during heavy rains, fed by a large number of streams.

The pattern of life in this region differs greatly from the nomadic pattern that prevails in most other parts of Sinai. The bulk of the Sinai's settled population lives in this northern region, concentrated in centers such as El-Arish, Rafah, and others. In fact, after Egypt recovered Sinai from Israel, intensive efforts were directed to encourage nomadic and seminomadic groups to settle down. As part of these efforts, special attention was given to develop agriculture and to reclaim land. A project is currently under way to reclaim about 400,000 *feddans* by introducing Nile water through a culvert under the Suez Canal. The total cultivable area in Sinai is estimated to be more than three million *feddans*, or about 40 percent of the total estimated cultivable area in present-day Egypt.

The region accommodates a variety of agricultural patterns that vary depending on the water supply. One pattern depends on rain – rare and uncertain – to grow large fields of barley, wheat and maize, with barley ranking first. When rain declines, large quantities of watermelon are grown. In other areas, underground water is used to grow fruits and vegetables seasonally on a large scale. The region also enjoys a wealth of palm trees that offer a considerable production of dates. Surprisingly, the Bedouin natives appear to have an unmatched natural ability to identify sites where underground water lies, and in marking the sites for the construction of dams to keep rainwater.

Thus, it can be safely stated that the development of fishing and agriculture in the northern parts of Sinai has been at the expense of pasturing, which is regarded as the traditional economic activity of desert inhabitants. Although there are no accurate statistics, there is justification in stating that the government's current policy encourages practices other than pasturing, including the development of farm animal plantations. The Egyptian-Israeli wars have, in fact, made Bedouins realize the importance of money that they could earn through practicing new activities rather than the meager earnings of pasturing.

Nevertheless, pasturing still represents an esteemed social value among the Sinai population. It is not surprising that the central region of Sinai is the most important region for pasturing as well as for the gathering of pastoral tribes; leading centers within are Al-Hasana and om-Nakhl. At the same time, pasturing does not preclude practicing agriculture wherever conditions allow, such as in the large number of scattered oases. But in all cases, the binding, overriding rule forbids pasturing on cultivated lands, in order to protect the crops and to avoid tribal conflicts. There are two kinds of pastures: first are those owned by a tribe, with identified borders and registered documentation; groups other than the owning tribe are not allowed to make use of such pastures. Second are open pastures that are commonly used by all tribes as long as crowding or conflict does not take place.

The daily and seasonal migration of the nomads in Sinai is practiced in pastoral areas without

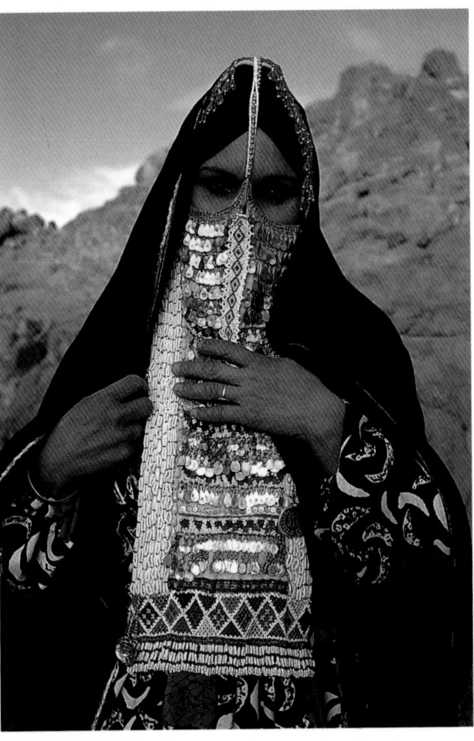

Above:
A Bedouin woman from the Midwest region wears a colorful Borko *to cover her face. Handmade from beads and stone, its color and decorations reveal tribe, marital status, social position and personal creativity.*

Following pages:
A valley in central Sinai illustrates the region's typical geography, combining mountains, sand, and sparse cultivable land. Note small planted areas.

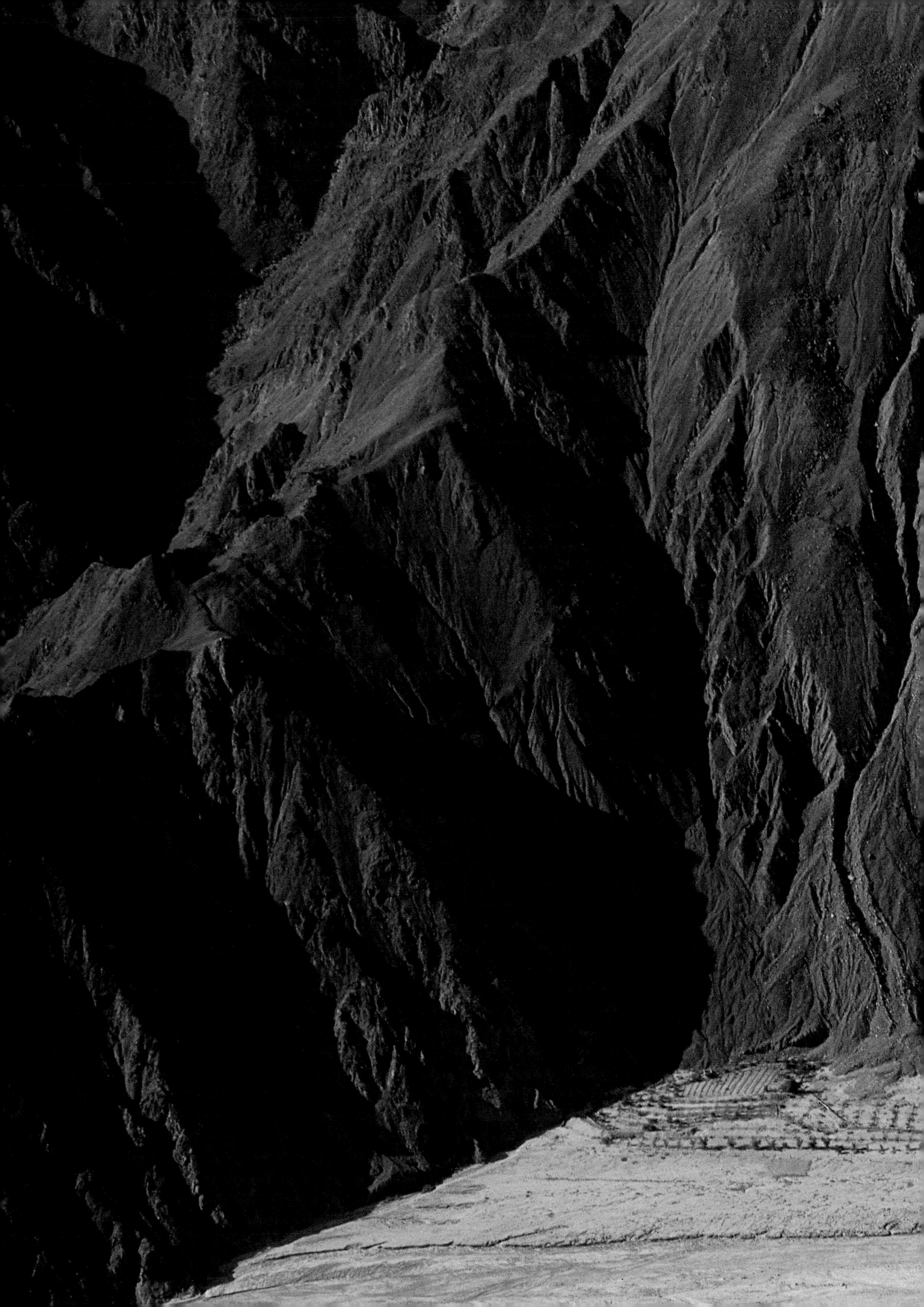

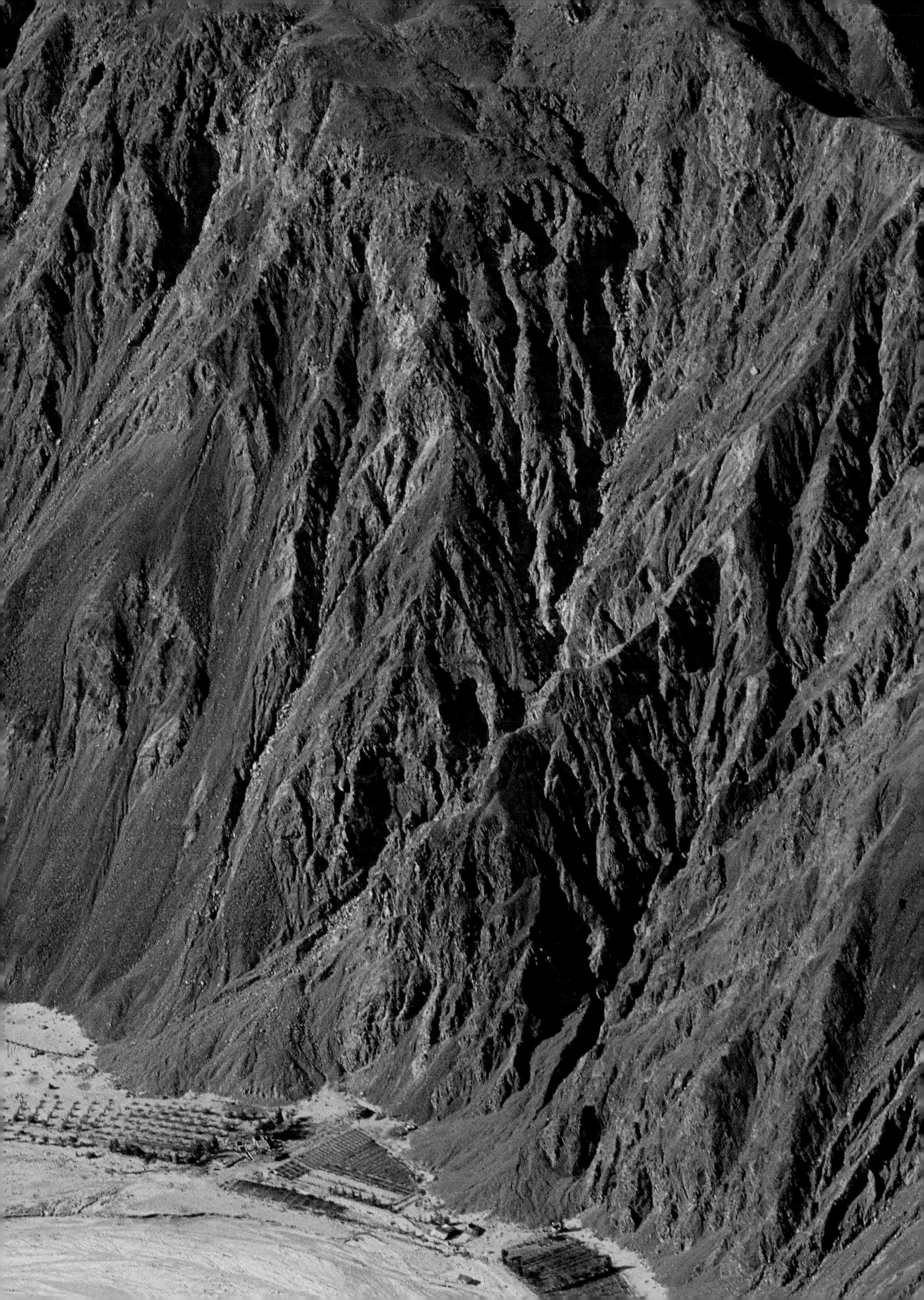

restriction or interference by the authorities, as long as they do not get too close to political boundaries, military areas or locations where multinational United Nations troops are encamped. Nomadic herds are usually mixed, rarely consisting of one kind of animal, and are commonly composed of sheep, goats and a smaller number of camels. Herds of camels need more care and usually run in areas that are farther away from settlements. In fact, camels occupy an eminent position and are considered a criterion of social prestige among Bedouins (see chapter starting on page 117). Generally, pasturing is losing ground as activities such as agriculture and tourism yield larger incomes, and more people shift, or at least hire others to do the pasturing for them. It can be easily noted that a drastic change is taking place among Sinai's inhabitants, from tending to live by subsistence, to a livelihood supported by a money economy.

In the northern region of Sinai we can witness how several patterns of life coexist and intermingle. Maritime, agricultural and desert environments have a combined influence on the life of the inhabitants, although each aspect retains, at least for now, its specific social, economic and political impact.

The rocky, mountainous two-thirds of Sinai to the south, constitutes a region that is ecologically very different from the North. Although the nomadic pattern of life prevails in the region, the presence of petroleum and ores such as manganese, gypsum, tafla and kaolin affects not only the population distribution within the region, but also social and economic practices.

A major factor that has added much to the change in the region during the last decade or so has been the development of large-scale tourism both along the Gulf of Suez and the Gulf of Aqaba, and in the region of St. Catherine's Monastery. Tourism has been stimulated not only by the adventure and recreation of the region, but by the incredible natural beauty on land and in the depths of seawaters surrounding the peninsula (see chapter starting on page 137). Thus, in this region of difficult terrain, a change in the modes of life is under way. The inhabitants of this region are managing to rise above the limitations set by nature, by learning how to turn nature's gifts to good account. In both northern and southern Sinai a significant change into more complex societies and economies is taking place.

The Concept of Isolating and Isolated Boundary

The Sinai Peninsula always has been regarded as Egypt's eastern shield against aggressors. Although very few people settled in Sinai, the peninsula witnessed waves of humanity that crossed it from east to west and from west to east. The fact that the peninsula was used mainly for passage into or out of Egypt was a result of its unattractive geographical features. However, the ancient Egyptian Pharaohs did not hesitate to send military campaigns into the peninsula from time to time to quell revolting Bedouins, or to set up operations to extract copper and topaz in the region. History also records Sinai as a transit station for Phoenician trade caravans traveling from the Phoenician coastland to their markets in Northwest Africa, a practice that encouraged and promoted trade between Egypt and the countries to the east as well as to the west.

With the progress of history, a wide range of threats to the basic security and political stability in the Nile Valley and Delta came from the east. Thus, it happened that Egyptians were forced to look upon Sinai as the eastern watchpoint of the valley, where the population was concentrated. The concept had its strong impact on the strategy of successive Pharaohs. Their defensive tactics could not simply end in Sinai proper, but had to extend beyond the peninsula itself, into the lands to the east in Palestine, the Levant and lands beyond.

The result was that Sinai continued to be reserved, more or less, for military purposes, with very little attention given to the promotion of life among the few native Bedouins. Later, the construction of the Suez Canal added further to that trend as it created a water barrier between the peninsula and the motherland. In all this, the human element played a dominant role in determining the relative importance of the peninsula to Egypt.

It is quite evident that the roles performed by Sinai throughout history reflected to a very great extent the limitations imposed by its desert environment. One example is that those who crossed the peninsula from east or west always limited their passage to the northern region where underground water was available. The peninsula itself remained an isolated region marked by vast stretches of sand and rock, heat, the absence or scarcity of water, thin and scattered forage, and difficult natural lines of communication. All these factors were allies of the desert dwellers, but at the same time made it difficult for the native to try to take his resources abroad. Thus, the scarce population of Sinai adapted to the difficult and isolated conditions they lived under.

Since 1948, Sinai has been the battlefield for four rounds of war between Egypt and Israel. In May 1948, the traditional roads and the railway line in northern Sinai were used to transport Egyptian volunteers and units of the armed forces into Palestine, where the first round of war took place. Hostilities were ended by the signing of the Rhodes Truce in 1949, yet the turmoil continued. In 1956, the peninsula was invaded by Israeli, British and French troops in retaliation for the nationalization of the Suez Canal. But, in 1957, Egyptian armed forces recovered their positions in Sinai and entered the Gaza Strip. The longest period of Israeli occupation of the peninsula came in 1967 when Egyptian armed forces were painfully defeated, caused mainly by corrupt and incompetent leadership. For the second time in ten years, the whole of Sinai came under Israeli occupation, lasting until 1973.

On October 6 that year, Egyptian forces staged an overwhelming victory over the Israelis. In an unprecedented crossing of the Suez Canal, they destroyed the Barlev defensive line along the eastern bank, and Sinai was recovered. Within the framework of Egyptian-Israeli peace agreements, the whole peninsula was recovered by Egypt in 1982, with the exception of the small site of Taba, which was recovered five years later through international arbitration. Thus Egypt restored its sovereignty over the entire peninsula. The war of October 1973 started a basic change in the political history of Sinai. It brought to an end the perception that the peninsula was a geographically isolated part of Egypt, of military importance alone. In fact, it took Egypt the long experience over several centuries to come to the present conclusion that the Sinai Peninsula is nothing less than an integral part of the motherland, with the same national rights and importance as other parts of the country.

The Concept of Integrated Region

The Egyptian leadership intended the October 1973 war to be the last war in the region. This intention was translated into a series of military and political steps that finally led to the complete withdrawal of Israeli troops from Egyptian territory, and the conclusion of a pioneering peace treaty between Israel and Egypt. This treaty is the promising cornerstone for establishing an overall peace settlement for which the Middle East has been striving for more than half a century.

The urgent question became: Could the 1973 war fulfill its main objective? Could the region enjoy a genuine, lasting and just peace after more than 25 years of hostilities and serious losses on all sides? The question stimulated a wide variety of answers, all of which had to revolve around the ideal interrelationship that needed to be founded and fostered between Egypt, the motherland, and Sinai. The experience of the past few decades makes it clear that modern sustained warfare is entirely out of the question. The enormous and destructive drain of continued warfare prevents improvement of the conditions under which many may survive and denies Sinai's enormous potential for development.

The political geography of Sinai once appeared to indicate a definite line of action on the part of contending powers. It seemed to be a sound policy to leave the peninsula as a theater reserved exclusively for war, and thus, if force must be exercised, it could be in strategic regions or strategic points where moves could be made with greater ease and flexibility. This use of military force to support a national policy could be termed a policy of "marginal control." Nevertheless, as Sinai's population and uses grew, it became clear that the peninsula could no longer be regarded solely as a territorial buffer between Egypt and its neighbors in the east, especially Israel. A new strategy had to be adopted that would take into consideration several important environmental and ecological conditions, based on the lesson of history that Sinai's rôle as a buffer zone proved to be purely passive.

Sinai's inhabitants, first of all, would have to adapt to the new situation, and take into consideration the extent of their new interrelations with outside communities resulting from the battlefield exchanges during the war years. An objective assessment would lead us to conclude that the natives now have a relatively wider range of historical, religious and traditional ties with their fellow citizens in the Nile Valley and Delta.

The strategy also must consider the potential for achieving integration, considering that such potential would be of greater impact within the framework of peace in the region. Again, a review of such potential would reveal the fact that Sinai's resources are abundant and economically exploitable. Significant additions to these resources can be realized by taking advantage of the motherland's water supplies, energy, skilled manpower, scientific research, capital and planners. The potential for exploiting the beauty and challenge of the peninsula for tourism is also very high.

The third point the strategy must consider is the presence of a national will to fulfill integration and to renounce old concepts of the peninsula as a buffer zone.

Opposite page:
Lush palm trees flourish in the Furtaga Oasis of South Sinai.

The Suez Canal, for example, has to be looked at simply as a waterway that crosses Egyptian territory, not as the northeastern limit of Egypt. It is reasonable to think that great emphasis is being put on the profound change that is taking place in the spiritual and mental attitudes, not only of Sinai's new population, but also of the inhabitants of the more densely populated regions of Egypt. Here, Sinai is one of the few regions in the world where the whole structure of social, economic and political life has been, and hopefully will continue to be, altered.

Generally speaking, a simple glance at the events taking place in the Middle East makes clear how complex and varied the region's problems are, and how far-reaching the decisions that must be translated into action by the Egyptian administration will be. Meanwhile, Sinai's economic and social problems embrace a region far beyond the peninsula itself. To elevate the standards of government there requires a continual examination of contemporary problems by all citizens, which brings new ideas, perceptions and independent judgments into the mix. This said, the problems following peace in the region will prove to be much more complicated than those of any preceding time. Among other things, the land and the elements of nature must be put to better economic use.

Thus, a new era in the history of Sinai began in October 1973. The peninsula has become an integrated part of Egyptian territory. Sinai is no longer reserved for military purposes; it is open to all Egyptians, the same as all other parts of the Republic.

Facing the Challenges of Development

Egypt faces a very serious challenge in overpopulation. Continued large annual increases in the population could drain much of the effort being made to develop the country's resources. Egypt's population multiplied six times from about 10 million at the beginning of the 20th century to an estimated 59 million in 1994. Although the annual rate of increase has dropped from 2.8 percent to 2.3 percent over the last two decades, this is still considered too high to permit targeted results to be achieved in economic and social development. But what makes this such a serious problem is that more than 98 percent of Egypt's population is concentrated within the limited area of the Nile Valley and Delta – less than 4 percent of the total area of the country. The limited resources of the Nile Valley and Delta are having to bear nearly the whole burden of the population increase.

Even worse is that the uneven geographical distribution of the population brought about a form of neglect of "remote" regions outside the Nile Valley and Delta. Development funds and programs in those regions were far behind the basic requirements needed to attract part of the population increase, and consequently they remained "remote" and thinly settled. It was only in the last decade or so that the government began extensive development programs in some of those regions within the overall national five-year plans of economic and social development.

Sinai is one of those "remote" regions, and its military status only added to its lack of development. Although Sinai occupies about six percent of Egypt's total area, its population did not exceed 125,000 a decade ago; at present it accommodates 225,000, or less than half of one percent of Egypt's population. Meanwhile, the potential for economic development in Sinai has proven to be both abundant and promising. After the peace agreement between Israel and Egypt, it seemed appropriate to consider the possibility of exploiting Sinai's resources with a view to making the region more attractive, and thus more able to contribute to the increase in the national income of the country as a whole, as well as to help the country face the problem of unemployment. Greater attention to the development of the region's resources also would conform with and foster the new strategy that looks upon Sinai as an integrated region of Egyptian territory. In brief, the peninsula is to play a genuine role in building up the future of the country.

The new policy of the administration promises a bright future for Sinai. The strategy aims not only at influencing the lives of the natives and helping them to shift into a settled and more productive form of living, but also at attracting reasonable numbers from the overpopulated regions within the Nile Valley and Delta. The objective of the administration is to have the peninsula accommodate about two million inhabitants by the end of this century and the beginning of the next.

A policy of such nature promises to provide productive jobs for about 500,000. New jobs will include a wide variety of activities in agriculture, fishing, raising herds, mining, tourism, and, last but not least, industry. In essence, this policy ultimately will help introduce a more economically and socially acceptable geographical distribution of the population in Egypt. It will also help achieve national goals for development, growth and progress.

Creating the migration of population from the Nile Valley to Sinai is a hard task. Though resources seem to be abundant and exploitable, and large areas of land and sites appear to be suitable for settlement, we have to keep in mind that the conditions of living in the peninsula are unusual and peculiar. We can hardly expect such areas to be occupied either rapidly or significantly until a scientific, technical and social plan of settlement comes into being. On the one hand, the administration has to determine the size of subsidy or incentive provided for the natives who become settlers, and what is socially and economically possible and desirable. On the other hand, the prospective settler should be provided with all the needed data concerning the conditions of life that he could face, along with definite information about more secure means to successfully carry out his intended activities.

The success of the administration's plan is not simply important, it is becoming vital. It can help the country to face the serious problem of its rapidly increasing population in an efficient manner and ultimately make development more fruitful, both socially and economically. This way, Egypt would open a gate through which it can escape the pessimistic presumption that the country could face a long period of continued recession.

Contributing to National Income

In spite of the fact that Sinai has very difficult environmental conditions, the peninsula also possesses a wealth of resources that would allow man, whether a native or a new settler from the Nile Valley, a positive measure of command over his difficult environment and allow him to enjoy all the amenities and benefits of a modern society. Recent applications provided sound illustrations of how the natives of Sinai can cope with a change that involves a more

Following pages:
An early sunrise shimmers on the Gulf of Aqaba. Across the waters, the mountains of Saudi Arabia begin to take shape.

elaborate and complex social organization than the one they lived under for many centuries. The elaborate economy that Sinai has started to enjoy can mean nothing but greater interdependence between its people and the rest of Egypt. Under the complex economy that is envisaged for Sinai by the administration, people in Sinai are to earn their livelihood in a number of different ways, ranging from primary production to the more complicated and advanced secondary and tertiary occupations. In all cases, man is to use skills and techniques that can enable him to meet as well as to master his environment.

In order to introduce the new strategy concerning Sinai, it was necessary to extend the administrative system applied in Egypt into the peninsula. Two measures were applied. First, the Suez Canal is not anymore to be regarded as a natural boundary separating the Sinai Peninsula from the rest of Egypt. The three administrative divisions lying on the west bank of the Canal—Port Said, Ismailia, and Suez—were to be expanded eastward to include considerable areas on the eastern bank of the Canal. Thus, the extreme western area of Sinai, looking on the Suez Canal, became integrated within three main Egyptian administrative divisions. The Suez Canal is not anymore a natural obstacle to the people on the west, nor is it the natural western limit of the peninsula.

The second measure within the new strategy was based on the principle that the larger remaining parts of Sinai could not be kept as "remote" or neglected areas. Thus, Sinai was divided into two administrative divisions: Northern Sinai and Southern Sinai. This new structure provided a clear introduction of the administration to all of the scattered communities within the peninsula, placing them within the reach of the various agencies concerned with services on the one hand, and with social and economic development on the other.

It was quite natural in the early stages of the new situation to give priority to the development of the infrastructure required for social and economic development of the peninsula. A network of paved roads has been constructed to connect the different parts of the peninsula and the rest of Egypt. This network of roads has proven a great benefit, not only to social and economic programs, but also to the tourist industry, which is becoming of great significance to the development of Sinai.

The main roads that the network covers start with the northern road that extends from Al Qantara, on the eastern bank of the Suez Canal to the north of Ismailia, to El-Arish and Rafah. The road passes through Bir El Abd and Al Nazar to the south of Lake Berdawil. From Al Qantara there is another road that runs southward along the Suez Canal, and opposite al-Timsah Lake the road runs eastward via Bir Gifgafa and Bir Rod Salim to Al Arija on the Israeli-Egyptian border.

At Suez, the tunnel of Ahmed Hamdi (named after an Egyptian martyr in the October 1973 war) was constructed under the Suez Canal in 1978 to facilitate, speed up, and promote traffic across the canal. Once the tunnel is crossed, the traveler has the choice of several roads that penetrate different parts of the peninsula, particularly the Southern Sinai administrative division. Among these roads the most important are: the road eastward through Mitla Pass, Nakhl, Al-Kontilla to the Egyptian-Israeli border and Taba; the road southward to Ras Sudr, Ras Matarma, Abu Zeneima, Abu Durba, El-Tor, Ras

Kanissa, to Sharm el Sheikh, and onward to Dahab, Nuweiba and Taba; and the road that branches from Abu Zeneima to Firan Oasis, hence via al-Watiaa Pass either to Nuweiba or to Dahab. This road passes by Gebal Musa and St. Catherine's.

Other than roads, attention has been given to the development of regular ferryboat service at several points along the Suez Canal. Studies have been completed recently on the possibility of constructing high bridges across the canal. A new, modern net of internal and international telephone exchanges has been developed to cover various sites in both Northern and Southern Sinai. Undoubtedly, the telephone service represents a basic tool for promoting tourism and other economic activities.

Several airports have been developed, some for international tourism. The most important are those at Sharm el Sheikh and El-Arish. At St. Catherine's, a smaller airport has been developed. Many other mining and administrative centers enjoy their own air-landing spots.

Generally speaking, the present networks of roads, airports, and telephone services have ended the isolation of Sinai and have made the region much smaller! Sinai is now prepared to start a new era as a region that can, and hopefully will, contribute significantly to Egypt's overall development.

The experience of the current few years indicates that Sinai is capable of playing quite an important role in the economic life of Egypt. In fact, the present contribution can be regarded as a reasonable step in that direction, especially since the peninsula possesses resources in a variety of domains.

Fishing and agriculture, as already mentioned, represent a form of integrated community mainly in the northern region. Although the future seems more promising by far, the present economic contribution of these industries is not trifling. The region exports more than 1,000 tons of the best quality fish, providing an income of not less than US$20 million of foreign currency per year. The region also produces a high quality of peaches, which are exported mainly to Arab Gulf countries.

Sinai is rich in mineral wealth and petroleum leads the list. The first oil discovery in Sinai was made in 1918 in Abu Durba in the central part of the eastern coast of the Gulf of Suez. The oil was found there near a surface seepage. The "field" was abandoned in the early 1920s when it became uneconomical to produce. After that, no exploration was undertaken until after World War II.

Since 1945, drilling has been resumed by a number of international oil companies. This resulted in the discovery of oil fields on land along the eastern coast of the Gulf of Suez, namely, Sudr, Asal, Ras Matarma, Feiran and Balayim East (Land). Offshore discoveries also were made. Of these, two offshore fields have their production, storage and shipping facilities installed along the west coast of Sinai. They are Balayim West (Marine) and Ras Badran. Some of these land oil fields, as well as Balayim Marine field, were exploited by Israel during the occupation of Sinai. By the late 1970s, an intensive plan for restoring proper exploitation was adopted.

The only gas discovery in Sinai was made in the area of Abu Ra'ad, to the southwest of Refah, which is now depleted.

The original recoverable oil reserves so far discovered in Sinai, including the above mentioned offshore fields, are about 2.6 billion barrels. The present average daily production from Sinai's fields is 270,000 barrels.

Sinai is also rich in a variety of ores. Top-quality manganese ore is produced in the region of Om Bagma, to the east of Abou Zeneima. An industry of ferro-manganese was started in 1980 at an annual output of 180,000 tons. Total reserves of manganese in the region amount to about 5.5 million tons. While the ore is found in several other scattered areas such as Sharm el Sheikh, further studies must determine if production is economic.

Kaolin, basic for the porcelain and china industry, is exploited in the region of Gebel Save Salama at about 45,000 tons per year. The ore also is important for other industries, such as thermo-brick, pipes, cement, textiles, paper, and rubber.

Annual production of white sands, used in the manufacture of glass and thermionics, amounts to about 30,000 tons, mainly in Abou Kafas, Nitch, and Bir el Nasab al Gharbi in the central plateau. Among other ores of economic importance are sulphur, phosphates, gypsum, limestone, marble, and black sand. Topaz is found in the region to the east of Abu Zeneima. Coal has been discovered in promising deposits and exploitation is starting.

A new resource for Sinai is tourism, which has recently invaded the life of the region. Although the tourist potential of the peninsula was first exploited in the late 1960s and early 1970s, its value has proven to be of great significance in the social and economic development of the peninsula. While the tourist industry as a whole has faced serious difficulties since 1990, tourism continued to flourish all over the different regions of Sinai. The northern sites are mainly oriented as summer resorts for domestic tourists. In the middle and south, sites are oriented to serve domestic tourists and those who come from various parts of the world, especially the United States, Western European countries, Japan and Israel. A large number of tourist villages and resorts have developed in numerous centers around the peninsula.

The success of the tourist industry in Sinai is due to a combined number of factors. The peninsula has a number of sites that enjoy an ancient religious prestige, and consequently are attractive to large numbers of tourists. A leading example is the region of the Monastery of St. Catherine and its surroundings. The peninsula also encompasses sites of great interest to those concerned with ancient history and archeology.

Geographically, the mountainous relief of the peninsula, with its large number of dissecting dry valleys, offers the visitor a unique and picturesque "natural gallery," where a combination of design, sculpture, carving and chiseling stand as witnesses to the glamour of nature and the magic power of erosion in shaping the surface of the earth. The peninsula also is surrounded by the sea, which presents the visitor a fascinating list of enjoyable sports, ranging from fishing, surfing and swimming to diving and underwater photography. There are large areas of beautiful coral fields, especially in the Gulf of Aqaba. The area of Ras Mohammad is kept as a natural reservation to protect the treasures of nature from the devastating cruelty of man.

Finally, the nomadic type of life that the natives lead offers the visitor an irresistible attraction, especially since those nomadic natives are scattered all over the peninsula. In addition, the Bedouin offer tourists a wealth of products that tell of the superior handicraft the natives possess.

Opposite page:
The clarity of the Red Sea water of Mersa Breka at Ras Mohammed illustrates why the southernmost tip of Sinai has become one of the world's most popular sports diving locales.

It is not strange that the peninsula has so rapidly acquired a priority position in the field of tourism.

In conclusion, while the economic development of Sinai is still in its early stages, the peninsula clearly is contributing significantly to the country's national income. Its contribution is not limited to one specific area, but is extensive within a wide variety of activities.

Science and the Future

The recent economic and social performance and trends in the Sinai Peninsula show clearly that it has every possible potential for even a more positive and fruitful future, based on self-reliance and self-sustainment.

At present, Egypt is implementing meaningful economic reforms at a speed that avoids jeopardizing social and political stability. Within the policy of the administration, the development of Sinai is a significant priority. Coping with this priority, the administration has recently established a high-level committee concerned with the future socioeconomic development of the peninsula.

Although it is a fact that certain geographical controls, notably those exerted by geology, relief and climate, always will persist and limit man's activities to some extent, it is also a fact that through experience, thought, discovery and invention man has learned to become less the slave of nature and more and more independent of his natural surroundings, ultimately to reach the stage where he can use nature for his own ends. Nevertheless, he cannot be the complete master of his environment, for in many cases nature still calls the tune.

Sinai stands as a good example of this struggle between man and nature. The experience of the last decade or so shows that as man develops his scientific knowledge, increases his understanding of his environment, and improves his technology, he is better able to wrest the secrets of nature from her and increasingly conquer and use nature for his own purposes. The previous review of the current conditions in Sinai show that the future is liable to offer man a lead over nature, especially since the present efforts have touched only a tiny portion of the peninsula's potential.

The socioeconomic development plans in Sinai aim at expanding the exploration of the peninsula's mining and petroleum resources, establishing industrial products, and enhancing the agricultural sector along with encouraging the organization of settled agricultural communities for Bedouins within a balanced environment and ecology. Such a balance is to be attained through the full exploitation of the region's natural potential and what it embraces of pastures, field and garden crops, medical herbs and plants, all within the proper use of a water supply that is very limited at present. All this is to be directed toward raising the density of the peninsula's population and converting it into a region that can attract significant numbers of the unemployed in the Nile Valley and Delta.

This plan of overall development has two major dimensions. First, there is the social dimension that aims at developing the Bedouin environment and the life of the Bedouin himself. Infrastructure and a variety of public services provided to settlement centers have proven to be quite effective. Second, the economic dimension is based on the development of water sources and agricultural development, including animal wealth; the application of modern technologies in the exploitation of mineral wealth and industrial activities; the development of fishing, especially in the northern region looking on the Mediterranean; and, finally, the development of tourism.

The concept of increasing man's ascendancy over his material environment in Sinai could stimulate a certain optimistic vision, as well as fiction, of what can take place in the future. Nevertheless, this optimistic vision may be justified by certain important undertakings. First, it is a requirement for the realization of such a vision to consider communication. The present network of roads and airports has brought the peninsula within easy reach, having overcome – to a certain extent – the mountainous barriers. Agricultural wealth will create new productive jobs for more than a half-million unemployed. Needless to say, the future agricultural exploitation of this region will necessitate the introduction of new technologies concerned with breeding quick-maturing varieties of plants and drought-withstanding species.

Along with the challenge of the water supply, the future faces the challenge of energy. New thermal and gas-electric stations have been constructed or are within the overall plan. What is even more promising is the construction of a grid to cover the whole peninsula, joined to the national grid before the close of the century. By then, a Mediterranean grid would be completed and the national grid will become part of it.

Once electricity potentials are examined, coal must be considered not simply as a possible source of energy, but also as an important competitive export. The discovery of coal deposits in the region of El Maghara and in Al-Rakb to its west, means wealth that is exploitable for more than 50 years, with reserves that exceed 37 million tons. Production is to start at about 125,000 tons per year. In five years, production is to increase to about 600,000 tons per year.

Once the peninsula is provided with the basic requirements of water, communication and electricity, it would be quite natural to adopt an optimistic view of the possibility to attract a wide variety of industries to the region, including small industries and handicrafts for natives. The vision involves the establishment of large industrial towns and parks, as well as several free-zones that can support the role to be played by Egypt in its economic incorporation in the Middle East.

Last, but not least, the future is liable to witness a far more striking boom in tourism. This prospect is based on a more proper and positive use of the glamour of this region, a feature present year-round.

One would tend to remember the American West during the past two centuries or so. With modern scientific innovations and the introduction of modern technologies, the rehabilitation of Sinai seems to be less overwhelming. It is quite safe to state that Sinai, which represented a burden to Egypt for centuries, will ultimately turn into a significant asset: socially, economically and politically.

The Religious Heritage of Sinai

by Dr. Gawdat Gabra

The peninsula of Sinai represents the crossroads of three religions, Judaism, Christianity and Islam. Beginning in very early times, the ancient Egyptians were attracted by the mineral deposits of Sinai and built a temple and some shrines there to worship their deities, the goddess Hathor, the "Mistress of Turquoise," and the god Sopd, the "Lord of the East." Thoth was also worshiped, together with some deified Pharaohs of the past, especially King Senefru.

Biblical Sinai is associated with the Exodus. According to the Koran, Moses went to Mount Horeb and lived for 40 years cleansing his soul in the solitude and tranquility of the desert of Sinai. God appeared to him in the miracle of the Burning Bush. Moses led the Israelites in the wilderness of Shur, the wilderness of Paran and the wilderness of Sin to reach the Mount of Horeb, Mount Sinai, where he received God's Law. With their miraculous history of God's revelation, these isolated places of Sinai were ideal for the exercise of a hermitic and monastic life. From the first centuries of Christianity, hermits began to congregate in the biblical sites of the Burning Bush, the Mount of the Law and the oasis of Pharan (Fayran) to devote themselves to a life of spiritual tranquility. The most famous monk in Sinai is John Climacus, the author of the distinguished work *The Heavenly Ladder*, who lived in the 6th century and developed a new type of spiritual exercise among the monks of Sinai.

Sinai is also associated with the Flight of the Holy Family into Egypt. The Holy Family crossed the Sinai Peninsula by taking the route that runs parallel to the shore of the Mediterranean Sea. Coptic tradition holds that the Holy Family stopped in Pelusium during the flight into Egypt.

The most important religious monument in Sinai is undoubtedly the famous Monastery of St. Catherine, which was built in the 6th century by the Byzantine Emperor Justinian and secured special privileges from the Prophet Mohammed. The tradition maintains that a delegation of the Monastery of St. Catherine went, in the year 625, to the Prophet asking his protection. They were accorded a hospitable reception by the Prophet and were granted a covenant of security; the original document was taken to Constantinople by Sultan Selim I in 1517. A copy is exhibited at the monastery.

Through Sinai to Egypt came the Arabs in 640 carrying the message of Islam to Africa, an event of immeasurable consequence in the shaping of history and culture in the region. One of the tenets of Islam is the pilgrimage to the holy city of Mecca. Until the 19th century, the methods of travel available to pilgrims were either sailing ships as far as Jedda or caravans. Caravans from Africa

Opposite page:
The head of the goddess Hathor adorns capitals of the temple in her name at Serabit El Khadem. A supreme goddess, protectoress of the rich mines on the lonely plateau, her temple was built and rebuilt over several hundred years.

Following pages:
Capitals with the heads of Hathor were among the finest in the temple of Serabit El Khadem. They are from the time of Thutmose III (1490-1439 B.C.), when many chambers, halls and pylons were added to the temple.

and Egypt used the Darb El Hajj or Pilgrims' Route, which lay across central Sinai. From the 13th century onwards, the caravans carried the *Mahmal* with the *Kiswa* from Egypt to Mecca. The *Mahmal* is a richly decorated palanquin or litter and the *Kiswa* is the silk cloth that hangs over the Kaaba.

The religious heritage of the Sinai Peninsula is highly respected by Jews, Christians and Muslims all over the globe.

The contribution of Sinai to the world's civilization is beyond estimation.

The Pharaonic Temple of Serabit El Khadem

The ancient Egyptians sent expeditions to Sinai to work the mines during the Old to the New Kingdom to acquire copper and turquoise. The main district of the mines are in the valleys of southwestern Sinai. Wadi El Maghara is situated to the west of Wadi Qenaia and at the north of Wadi Mokkattab. Its mines were the first to be exploited. Many rock inscriptions bear witness to the Egyptian mining activities there. The earliest inscription dates to King Zoser (2700-2680 B.C.). The last attested Old Kingdom expedition in Wadi El Maghara was that of King Pepi II (2290-2203 B.C.). Many reliefs represent great Old Kingdom Pharaohs, such as Senefru, Cheops, Sahure and Pepi II, smiting the Asiatics. Although some kings of the Middle Kingdom (2040-1785 B.C.) and of the New Kingdom (1552-1069 B.C.) are attested in Wadi El Maghara, the site never regained its former importance.

The most important Egyptian mining activities are in Serabit El Khadem with its Temple of Hathor. The significance of this site begins with the 12th Dynasty (1991-1785 B.C.), at the time when the mines of Wadi El Maghara were falling into disuse. There is no evidence that the ancient Egyptians knew the site of Serabit El Khadem before the beginning of the 12th Dynasty. The earliest part of the temple seems to have been a modest affair. It is a small rock-cut "Cave of Hathor," preceded by a court and a portico, which dates to the beginning of the 12th Dynasty. Another sanctuary belongs to the same period and was renewed during the reign of King Ramses IV. The temple buildings carry us without break through the 12th Dynasty. The 18th Dynasty (1552-1295 B.C.) saw a considerable change in the form and direction of the temples; the axis was turned through an angle so that all later additions to the temple were made on a new orientation. A shrine dedicated to Sopd was built and the Temple of Hathor was much enlarged; many chambers, halls and the pylon were constructed during the time of Queen Hatshepsut and King Thutmose III. Only a few additions were made to the temple buildings in the 19th and the 20th dynasties. Ramses VI (1144-1136 B.C.) is the last ruler who left his name in the temple.

At Serabit El Khadem, Hathor was a supreme goddess. In most cases she is described as the "Mistress of Turquoise." She is also "Mistress of the Lapis Lazuli" and "Mistress of the Good Color," i.e., the good color of the turquoise. Many scenes show the king making an offering to Hathor, sometimes accompanied by officials, as on the great pylon where King Thutmose III is depicted making an offering accompanied by his two officials Sennefer and Kenena. The pillars, with heads of the goddess Hathor from the time of Thutmose III, are the finest in the temple. The god next in importance after Hathor was Sopd, who is always described as "Lord of the East" and only once as "Sopd of the foreign lands." Some other gods occur on the monuments of Serabit El Khadem, of these the most significant are Thoth and the deified King Senefru.

The Exodus

That an exodus occurred need not for a moment be doubted. But the biblical account of the Exodus dates from long after the event, and despite the researches of many scholars in biblical Sinai, we are not in a position to determine what route the Hebrews really followed, except in conjecture. It is difficult to estimate the number of Israelites who left Egypt. It has been suggested that the number of about two million (Exodus 12:37) might be greatly reduced by translating the word *alaf*, generally rendered "thousands," as "families"; thus the number may have been about 27,000. The escape of the Israelites from Egypt was undoubtedly less important to the Egyptians than to those who left. In the following lines we find the only mention of the name Israel in Egyptian texts, inscribed on a stela from the time of the Pharaoh Merenptah (c. 1224-1214 B.C.):

The princes lie prostrate saying "Hail!"
Not one lifts his head among the Nine Bows;
Destruction for Libya: Hatti is pacified;
Canaan is plundered with every evil;
Askelon is taken; Gezer is captured;
Yanoam is made nonexistent;
Israel lies desolate; its posterity is no more;
Hurru has become a widow for Egypt.

There is no evidence to identify with certainty any of the ancient Egyptian kings with the "Pharaoh of the oppression." Some scholars agree that Merenptah or his father, the famous King Ramses II (1279-1212 B.C.) was the Pharaoh of the Exodus; others prefer to identify him with Thutmose III (1479-1425 B.C.), Amenhotep II (1425-1401 B.C.), or Amenhotep III (1390-1325 B.C.). It is, however, very possible that the Exodus occurred during the time of the Hyksos; they were tribes from western Asia who ruled Egypt for a period of nearly a hundred years (c. 1650-1553 B.C.). It has been fairly established that Avaris, the capital of the Hyksos, and Piramesse, the Delta residence of the Ramessides, are to be located in Tell el Dabaa-Khatana-Quantir in East Delta. Pithom (Heroonpolis), one of the cities the captive Israelites are alleged to have built for the Pharaoh, is identified by many scholars with Tell el-Maskhuta in Wadi Tumilat. Twenty kilometers south of Suez is Ain Musa, the Spring of Moses, where according to tradition the Hebrew tribes made their first stop after crossing the Red Sea. Wadi Fayran, where the biblical Rephidim seems to be located, was occupied by the Amalekites, and it was here where the battle between they and the Israelites was fought. Before the entrance to the Fayran Oasis, one passes a large granite rock; tradition holds that this rock was the one that yielded water when struck by Moses. The site is dominated by Gebel Serbal, an imposing high mountain that stands alone on the plain. Early hermits thought at first that from this mountain the Law was delivered. Finally the children of Israel reached the sacred Mount Horeb, where Moses received God's Law. Scholars identify Mount Horeb with Mount Sinai, which is called Gebel Musa or "Mount Moses." The Plain of El-Raha, to the west of Gebel Musa is generally accepted as the traditional campground of the

Following page:
Gebel Musa or Mount Moses, the biblical Mount Sinai where Moses received God's Law, climbs 2,285 meters high in a region of South Sinai, home to several similarly high peaks. The Monastery of St. Catherine is situated on a shoulder of Mount Sinai. To the west is the Plain of El-Raha, where the Israelites fleeing Egypt camped while Moses communed with God on the mountaintop.

Facing page:
Moses Removing his Sandals before the Burning Bush, *11th century. Tempera on panel, 92 x 64 cm.*

The Monastery of St. Catherine boasts the largest collection of icons in the world, more than 2,000 from the 6th century to the present. This priceless icon depicts the site where the monastery was eventually built.

Israelites while Moses communed with God on the summit of the mountain.

The exact route of the Exodus is still the subject of controversy among biblical scholars. We do not know where the Israelites believed the wilderness of Shur, the wilderness of Sin and the wilderness of Paran began and ended. However, beginning in early times, the holy places of Sinai, including the broad Plain of El-Raha and Mount Sinai, attracted many pilgrims. Visitors, pilgrims and scholars will continue to admire and to seek out these places where the history of three major religions unfolded.

The Monastery of St. Catherine

The Monastery of St. Catherine is situated on Wadi el-Dayer below the shoulder of Mount Sinai; to the west is the Plain of El-Raha. Since the 4th century, this mountain has been generally accepted as the biblical Mount Horeb, where Moses received the tablets of the Law with the commandments, and the spot on which the monastery was built has been venerated as the site of the Burning Bush.

The Monastery of St. Catherine is undoubtedly the world's most important and interesting monastery. It is one of the very few early Christian building complexes that have not been destroyed or reconstructed and restored several times over the centuries. The monastery's spiritual heritage is beyond estimation. Its architecture, mosaics, wall paintings, icons, historical documents, codices and illuminated manuscripts represent great treasures of the world's legacy. By the early 4th century many anchorites and hermits were attracted to Mount Sinai, seeking silence, isolation and cleansing of the soul. They settled in monastic communities near the site of the Burning Bush. According to tradition, St. Helena, the mother of St. Constantine, ordered in 337 the construction of a chapel on that site. The first mention of a small church in the valley of the Burning Bush is made between 373 and 381 by the Egyptian anchorite Ammonius; this has been confirmed through archeological investigations near the site. But the main history of the monastery began with the foundation of the great Church of the Transfiguration of the Savior and the building of the strong enclosure wall by Emperor Justinian sometime between the years 548 and 565. Antonius of Placenta visited the monastery around 570 and observed many monks carrying crosses and singing psalms; there were also three abbots with great knowledge of Latin, Greek, Coptic and Syriac. By that time the monastery had gained international reputation. Men of distinction have served as monks in Sinai, such as Gregory I, Patriarch of Antioch (570-593), and John Climacus. Pope Gregory the Great (590-604) provided the monastery with many gifts and built a hospital there.

After the Arab conquest of Egypt in 641, the monks continued to live in their monastery unmolested and unscathed, especially during the early Islamic period. According to tradition, the monks sent a delegation to Medina, in 625, asking for Prophet Mohammed's protection. He granted them the famous *Achtiname Testament*, which protected the monks from danger and exempted them from heavy taxation. A copy of this document is exhibited in the monastery. In 1517 Sultan Selim took the original document to Constantinople to enrich his collection of firmans. The tolerance of most of the Muslim rulers, who in general respected the monastery, is attributed to the

Opposite page:
The Heavenly Ladder, *early 12th century. Tempera on panel, 41 x 29.5 cm.*

The 30 rungs of the ladder in this icon illustrate the 30 virtues the monks must acquire and that it's not always easy to maintain the upward climb. John Climacus, the religious philosopher and abbot of St. Catherine's reaches paradise first, followed by Antonius, the first bishop of Sinai.

Pages 84-85:
A small community of monks inhabit the tiny Monastery of St. Catherine that is nestled in the slopes of Mount Sinai. Anchorites and hermits were attracted to the site from the early days of Christianity. The monastery's foundation and the building of the strong enclosure wall was begun by Justinian in the 6th century.

Pages 86-87
Another view shows the monastery at the foot of a great pink granite mass of the sacred mountain.

Prophet's testament and this is one of the main reasons that the monastery's monumental collection of icons, manuscripts and other treasures has been preserved. By the early 8th century the monastery had become an independent bishopric and then an archbishopric after the abolition of the bishopric of Pharan. Constantine, bishop of Sinai, participated in the fourth great church synod of 869 in Constantinople. It is worthy of note that the Church of Sinai is the smallest independent church of the Orthodox Communion. It is ruled by the "Archbishop of Mount Sinai," the abbot of the Monastery of St. Catherine. In the middle of the 10th century the monastery suffered from Bedouin pillage. The rise in the international significance of the monastery was closely associated with the transference of the relics of St. Catherine to the Sinai monastery in the 10th century. In the 11th century, the Monastery of the Transfiguration changed its name in honor of St. Catherine.

St. Catherine was a virgin martyred at Alexandria in the early 4th century. Her following began in the 9th-10th century at Mount Sinai, to which her body was supposed to have been transported by angels. Legend represents her as of a noble family and of exceptional learning. Because of her faith and her protest against the persecution of Christians by Maxentius, she was tied to a wheel – later called *Catherine's wheel* – and tortured; but the machine broke down, injuring bystanders. Finally St. Catherine was beheaded.

There was great devotion to her in the Middle Ages, especially in France. The celebrated Simeon of the "Five Tongues," a monk of Sinai, went to Europe to collect alms for the monastery. He bestowed numerous relics of St. Catherine upon the charitable donors and his mission was extremely successful.

In the beginning of the 12th century the monks, in a fine show of religious amity, authorized conversion of the old monastery's refectory to a mosque provided with a square minaret. Any threat, especially under the Mamluks, was dispelled through that concession to the Islamic world around the monastery. During the early Middle Ages, the monastery flourished; some travelers observed thousands of monks living in its vicinity, including Copts, Armenians, Ethiopians and Gregorians. Thousands of pilgrims came from Europe to Mount Sinai, as a part of their Holy Land pilgrimage, to be blessed at the monastery. The Crusader presence encouraged the flow of pilgrims. Although the monks were granted the protection of the Latin Kingdom in Jerusalem, they avoided exciting suspicion. So when Balduin I (1085-1118), king of Jerusalem, wanted to visit the monastery, they managed to dissuade him from visiting their territory. The monastery was in a very remarkable position: its ties with Byzantium were imperishable and it was more closely linked with the sees of Jerusalem and Constantinople than with the Greek Orthodox Church of Alexandria. Located on Egyptian soil, it was protected by Egyptian rulers.

The monastery's international reputation remained great throughout the world. Princes of Europe have shown respect to the monastery and were often ready to help during difficult times when religious differences between East and West led to acts of fanaticism. Despite the schism between the Roman and the Orthodox churches, Pope Honorius III (1216-1227) issued a bull in which he confirmed Simeon as bishop over Mount Sinai and the

Opposite page:
A bas-relief in a cross motif adorns the south enclosure wall of St. Catherine's Monastery.

neighboring estates in the East. In the beginning of the 13th century the monastery increased its external properties, especially in Crete.

The Ottoman invasion of Egypt by Sultan Selim in 1517 did not affect the status of the Monastery of St. Catherine. The monks succeeded in securing more privileges and the monastery increased its external holdings in Russia, Crete, Wallachia and Moldavia (modern Romania), and it maintained considerable cultural activities with these regions. In the 17th century the monastery managed to extend its educational activities to Crete, including a school at Herakleion.

During the time of the French campaign in Egypt (1798-1802), the monastery's north wall was restored after its collapse by heavy and long rain in December 1798. Napoleon's significant contribution to the monastery is the Kleber Tower, named after his representative in Egypt. He also issued a declaration of protection December 19, 1798, by which the privileges of the monastery were confirmed. Mohammed Ali (1805-1848) allowed the monks a percentage of customs dues levied in Cairo to support their monastery.

One of the old traditions of the monastery is the philanthropy of the monks, mainly through their distribution every morning of free rations of unleavened bread to the Bedouin tribe, the Gebeliya. In 1966 the representatives of the Orthodox Church and Constantine, the ex-king of Greece, celebrated the 1,400th anniversary of the monastery. On the wild, barren and arid but incredibly beautiful mountains of southern Sinai, the monks of this monastery have continued their spiritual and cultural activities for many centuries and it is very moving to hear today their supplication, sung as it has been every day since the 6th century: "...on behalf of the founder of this Holy Monastery, our pious Emperor Justinian and Empress Theodora of blessed memory."

The Enclosure Wall

During many periods the desert nomads of Arabia used Mount Sinai as a covert to infiltrate into Palestine. The hermits living there appealed to Emperor Justinian to shelter them. The account of the Byzantine historian Procopius concerning the foundation of the monastery is as follows:

"In what was formerly called Arabia and is known as 'Third Palestina,' a barren land extends for a great distance, unwatered and producing neither crops nor any useful thing. A precipitous and terribly wild mountain, Sina by name, rears its height close to the Red Sea, as it is called.... On this Mt. Sina live monks whose life is a kind of careful rehearsal of death, and they enjoy without fear the solitude which is very precious to them. Since these monks have nothing to crave – for they are superior to all human desires and have no interest in possessing anything or in caring for their bodies, nor do they seek pleasure in any other thing whatever – the Emperor Justinian built them a church which he dedicated to the Mother of God, so that they might be enabled to pass their lives therein praying and holding services. He built this church, not on the mountain's summit, but much lower down. For it is impossible for a man to pass the night on the summit, since constant crashes of thunder and other terrifying manifestations of divine power are heard at night, striking terror into man's body and soul. It was in that place, they say, that Moses received the Law from God. And at the base of the mountain this Emperor built a very strong fortress and established there a

considerable garrison of troops, in order that the barbarian Saracens might not be able from that region, which, as I have said, is uninhabited, to make inroads with complete secrecy into the lands of Palestine proper."

Procopius' account must not lead to the conclusion that Justinian's motive was monastic and military, as part of a defensive system to protect the Empire; for the enclosure wall is not provided with effective flanking towers. Its four towers are simple reinforcements of the corners. However, the enclosure wall was strong enough to let the monks feel safe, especially considering that the Bedouin are naturally incapable of storming such a thick wall. The enclosure wall is of granite, a building material that is locally available. It can be traced throughout the entire perimeter despite the many later superstructures. The battlements are still in position in many parts of the outer wall. In some places the walls reach the height of 30 meters; this is owing to the uneven ground on which the monastery was built. Many of the stones that are not above slit windows, are carved with panels. They date from the 6th century when Justinian ordered the monastery erected. The main original entrance is at the northwestern wall. It has been walled up. To the left is a small postern with an 18th-century porch, which is still in use as an entrance to the monastery.

The original plan of the Church of the Transfiguration was smaller than the present church. It was built in the shape of a three-aisled church with an apse turned to the east. Later, before the Arab conquest of Sinai, the narthex – a vestibule or entrance hall to a basilica usually located at the west end – the lateral rows of rooms, and the Chapel of the Burning Bush were added. One approaches the church by descending a flight of steps that leads down to the western entrance of the narthex. Its massive wooden door dates from the time of the Fatimides, in the 11th century. One of its carved panels shows the Transfiguration of the Savior. In the narthex a wonderful collection of icons is displayed. The great cypress-wood doorway, which leads into the nave, is one of the most significant of a few existing doors from the Byzantine period in Egypt. Its panels are carved with splendid animals, birds and plants. The nave has two rows of six columns, each of them surmounted by a differently carved big capital of local granite, nearly one meter high. They support arches above which is a row of rectangular windows. Although many elements were added to the nave, such as the iconostasis – a screen on which icons are placed and which separates the sanctuary from the rest of the church – ceiling panels, pulpit and chandeliers, it still preserves the atmosphere of original monumentality. The ceiling panels conceal a series of the original 13 roof trusses. According to carbon-14 tests, they belong to the 6th century. The first beam from the west and the two central beams bear inscriptions. They are of special significance for the history of the monastery as they mention Emperor Justinian as living, and his wife, Empress Theodora, as deceased. Thus the church must have been built between 548 and 565. We are also informed that the architect of the nave was Stephanus of Alia, a Nabatean. The bottom surfaces of the beams are not concealed by the later panels. They are decorated with exquisite 6th-century carvings representing floral ornaments and animals as well as sea creatures and nilotic scenes.

Each of the two side aisles of the

Opposite page:
Wooden door carving, Fatimid period (11th century).

The Prophet Zacharias stands in the center of this carved panel that adorns a cypress wood door of the church at the Monastery of St. Catherine.

Pages 92-93
The church nave is flanked on either side by a row of six columns, each surrounded by carved capitals of local granite almost one meter high. Ceiling panels conceal the original 13 roof trusses, which have been carbon-dated to the 6th century. Three of them bear inscriptions dating construction between 548 and 565.

Pages 94-95
The main section of the gilded iconostasis*– the icon laden screen that separates the sanctuary from the rest of the church– contains many holy images painted by Jeremiah Palladas of Crete. The screen itself was carved in 1612. To the left, the icon of the* Virgin and Child *is accompanied by figures of Kings David and Solomon and the Prophets Isaiah and Daniel; to the right is* Christ Enthroned *with symbols of the evangelists; on the doors in the middle are figures of the Prophets Moses and Aaron. The whole iconostasis can be seen toward the rear of the photograph on pages 92-93.*

Pages 96-97
The Transfiguration, *absidal mosaic, mid-6th century.*

This mosaic is one of the greatest treasures of St. Catherine's Monastery. It depicts Christ at the Transfiguration. Standing to His right is Moses; to His left, is the Prophet Elijah; kneeling to the left and right are the Apostles John and James, while Peter is prostrate before Him. On the cornice, medallions depict the apostles, including the evangelists Luke, Mark and Matthew, and the prophets St. John Chrysostom, King David and the Abbott Longinus. The mosaic, located in the apse of the church, ranks among the most important masterpieces of early Byzantine art. It can be glimpsed in the upper background of the photo on pages 92-93. A second mosaic in the church is titled Moses Receiving the Tablets of the Law at the Burning Bush. *Both artworks were probably executed by a Constantinople atelier under the personal patronage of the Emperor Justinian.*

Ἀπρίλιος.

Μάρτιος.

+ Ο ΗΛΙΑC
+ Ο ΙΩΑΝΝΗC

+ΜΩΥCΗC
+ΙΑΚΩ ΒΟC
+ ΠΕΤΡ ΟC
ΠΑ Υ ΛΟC
ΦΙ ΛΙΠ ΠΟC
ΘΩ ΜΑ C
ΜΑ Τ ΘΕ ΟC
ΘΑ ΔΔ ΔΕ ΟC
ΜΑ ΘΙ ΑC

Opposite page:
Christ Pantocrator, *first half of the 6th century.*
Encaustic icon, 84 x 45.5 cm.

church has a flat roof and a row of windows. The side aisles are flanked by lateral rows of rooms that extend the length of the north and the south wall of the church. The rooms have small apses with adjoining service niches. They are used today as side chapels, but their original purpose is not clear. The sanctuary is at the east end of the nave. It is separated from the nave by an impressive, gilded iconostasis, which was carved in 1612. Its icons were painted by the Cretan artist Jeremiah Palladas. The four panels of the iconostasis bear large icons of St. John the Baptist, the Holy Virgin Mary, Christ and St. Catherine. At the center of the sanctuary stands the original marble altar encased in an 18th-century housing of marquetry. Two original panels of marble are preserved from the screen that formerly enclosed the sanctuary. Their fine relief represents two confronting deer flanking a cross. The tomb of St. Catherine is on the south of the sanctuary. On the pilasters that flank the apse are two painted panels; the panel on the pilaster to the left depicts the Sacrifice of Isaac, on the right, behind the tomb of St. Catherine, the Sacrifice of Jephtah's Daughter. Apparently, both scenes belong to the 7th century. They are intended to presage Christ's sacrifice.

The half dome of the sanctuary and the wall above it are decorated with magnificent 6th-century mosaics. They are the monastery's great treasures, and rank amongst the most important masterpieces of early Byzantine art. The mosaics would have been originally visible for the full length of the nave, immediately confronting the beholder when he entered the church. The view into the apse is obstructed by the 17th-century iconostasis and the chandeliers. The mosaics of the apse depict the *Transfiguration of the Savior*, and *Moses Receiving the Tablets of the Law at the Burning Bush*. The original dedication of the church and its special function are indicated by these mosaics: the church was intended to commemorate the transfiguration of Christ, which was attended by Moses, who was associated with Mount Sinai.

When the visitor looks at the Transfiguration, the scene will appear like a huge eye with Christ standing within the mandorla as the pupil, figures standing out in wonderful shades of blue, red and green against the gold ground. Christ is flanked by Moses at the right and Elijah at the left. John and James are kneeling; the recumbent Peter is under the mandorla. The Transfiguration is framed by two rows of medallions; the ones above contain bust-like portraits of the twelve apostles. Peter, John and James, who appear in the Transfiguration, are replaced by the two Evangelists Luke and Mark and by Matthias. Prophets of the Old Testament are represented below. The medallion in the upper-middle shows the Cross; the one below, in the midst of the prophets, shows King David. The medallions in the corner contain the portraits of two monks. The one at the right is Longinus, the monastery's abbot, in whose reign the mosaic was made; at the left is the Deacon John. Both are depicted with a square nimbus, indicating that they were still living at the time of the execution of the mosaic. The spandrels are occupied by a scene representing two flying angels with peacock wings. They offer the scepter and the orb to the lamb. The lower parts of the spandrels contain two medallions, with the Virgin Mary to the right and John the Baptist to the left. The wall above the vault is decorated with two scenes from the life of Moses to the left and right of a pair of arched windows. In the left scene,

he is shown loosening his sandals before the Burning Bush, and in the right, he receives the Tablets of the Law from the hands of God in the form of a scroll.

The great artist who was responsible for the execution of these mosaics must have belonged to a Constantinople atelier and have been supported by the personal patronage of Emperor Justinian, the founder of the monastery. The mosaics of Sinai are the only pure, preserved mosaics from the Justinianic age, unlike those of Ravenna which are influenced by the Italian style.

Aetheria, an aristocratic lady from Spain, visited Mount Sinai towards the end of the 4th century. Her careful record of her travel includes an account about the Burning Bush. She says: "It was furthermore necessary to go out at the head of the valley, because there were many cells of hermits, and a church, where the bush is; this bush is alive to the present day and sends forth shoots. This is the bush I spoke of above, out of which God spoke to Moses in the fire. Where the bush stands in front of the church there is a very pleasant garden."

The Chapel of the Burning Bush is considered the holiest of the holy in the monastery. It lies below and behind the eastern apse of the nave. It is accessible through the doors of the two pastophoria, the sacristies adjoining the apse. Until the Middle Ages a growing bush believed to be the original bush stood in a court adjoining the church's apse. The German Magister Theitmer, who visited Sinai in 1216, tells us that the bush had been taken away and divided among Christians for relics, and a chapel stood in the sacred spot. It is not known when the Chapel of the Burning Bush was built. However, its masonry is very similar to the building style of the 6th century, and it must therefore have been built in the 6th-7th century, before the Arab conquest of Palestine and Sinai. The altar stands in the small apse over a slab, which marks the original spot of the bush. In the apse is a mosaic of a cross, which dates from the 10th century. The walls of the chapel are clad in beautiful blue-green-white Damascene tiles and decorated with icons.

The old refectory lies near the southeast corner of the church; it is difficult to ascertain its original purpose. It is a rectangular room, roofed with Gothic painted vaulting, and dates to the 12th-13th centuries. In the apse at the eastern side is a wall painting from 1573 representing the Judgment Day.

Below is another mural depicting the Hospitality of Abraham (1577). In the room stands a long wooden table with a beautiful 18th-century carving of angels and flowers. Many of the medieval pilgrims scratched their names on the walls of this room.

The bell tower was built in the 19th century by Gregorius, a Sinai monk. The campanile on the left-hand tower was presented by Russia in 1871.

Treasured Manuscripts

The library of the monastery is one of the richest monastic libraries in the world. It contains more than 4,000 manuscripts – about 3,000 of them in Greek and several hundred in Arabic, Syriac, Gregorian, Armenian, Coptic, Ethiopian and Slavic. In addition, there are approximately 5,000 books, some of them produced not long after the invention of printing. Most of the manuscripts deal with theological, liturgical and historical subjects. The library boasts a collection of historical documents issued by emperors, patriarchs and bishops. Apart from the testament of the Prophet, the library preserves many original firmans, or decrees, in which the caliphs and sultans of Islam promised protection for the monks of St. Catherine.

Today the *Codex Syriacus* is the most important manuscript preserved in the library. It is from the 5th century and contains parts of the New Testament. But the greatest treasure, which had been protected for many centuries by the monks of the monastery, is undoubtedly the celebrated *Codex Sinaiticus*, which was removed from St. Catherine's in the last century. Since this codex predates the erection of the monastery, it is very probable that a monk who came to live at Mount Sinai brought it with him. However, it is well known that during the Middle Ages many monks flocked to the monastery with such invaluable treasures.

The *Codex Sinaiticus* was discovered by Konstantin Tischendorf. On a visit in 1844, he found some leaves of the Old Testament books, but it was not until a later visit in 1859 that he saw the New Testament and recognized its great value. The codex dates probably to the later 4th century. Besides the Old Testament, it contains the whole New Testament as well as the "Epistle of Barnabas" and parts of the "Shepherd of Hermas." Tischendorf was allowed to take the codex to Cairo for further study and he finally took it to Europe and placed it in the hands of the Russian czar. The manuscript was never returned to Sinai and found its way to the Imperial Library at St. Petersburg. The Soviet government sold it in 1933 for 100,000 English pounds to the British Museum. In 1975 a dozen of the missing leaves of the codex were found in a hoard of varied manuscripts discovered in the monastery. They remain at St. Catherine's. In the British Museum are 346 leaves and a fragment; 43 leaves are preserved in Leipzig.

The library contains also a number of valuable illuminated manuscripts that have made important contributions to the study of iconography.

The Icon Collection

With its 2,000 icons the Monastery of St. Catherine boasts the largest collection of icons in the world. Many of these priceless icons are unique and of great spiritual and artistic value. A part of the collection represents some of the finest works of the early Byzantine period. The icons of the monastery were not affected by the iconoclastic controversy of the 8th and 9th centuries – when the icons in Byzantium were destroyed – as Sinai became an Islamic territory about 640. Icons were objects of veneration rather than displayed for their aesthetic values. They played a significant role in the public as well as in the private worship of the Greek Church. In the East, icons are accorded all the proper signs of veneration, such as kisses and incense; many icons have been famous for their miracles. Some of the pious pilgrims who visited the monastery at Sinai spoke of miracle-working icons that were hanging on the walls of the aisles of the basilica or on the iconostasis.

The icons of the Monastery of St. Catherine bear witness to the long history of this monastery. In no other place can icons from the 6th century on be studied in an uninterrupted way. The artistic value of icon treasures preserved at St. Catherine's is beyond estimation. Some of the works were painted there; others exemplify the stylistic trends of important centers of icons in the Byzantine Empire. The so-called Cretan school flourished after the fall of Constantinople in 1453 and

Following pages:
Virgin and Child between St. Theodore and St. George, *6th century. Encaustic icon, 68 x 49 cm.*

St. Peter, *second half of the 6th century, first half of the 7th. Encaustic icon, 92.8 x 53.*

Above:
The Three Hebrews in the Furnace
6th century.
Encaustic icon, 35.5 x 49.6 cm.

Opposite page:
St. Nicholas, *10th century.*
Tempera on panel, 43 x 33.1 cm.

This is probably the earliest icon. The medallions decorating the frame represent Christ, between Peter and Paul at the top, and soldier and physician saints.

continued until the end of the 17th century. Although four icons from St. Catherine's were known to the scholarly world since the middle of the 19th century, it was not until the 1950s that Professor Kurt Weitzmann prompted the universities of Princeton, Michigan and Alexandria to undertake five expeditions to study this great heritage in collaboration with Greek scholars.

The oldest and rarest icons, dating to the 6th and 7th centuries, are executed in the encaustic technique, using heated wax colors. This technique was used in different parts of the Hellenistic world and was beautifully applied on the many portraits of Fayyum in Egypt.

The icon of Christ Pantocrator represents Christ as ruler of the world, and is the work of a superior artist. Jesus holds with his left hand a jewel-studded, thick Gospel book; the right hand is blessing. Christ Pantocrator is characterized by full parted hair falling on the left shoulder. The outstanding artistic quality of this 6th century icon points to a Constantinopolitan work.

Another work of a great artist is the 6th century icon (h. 68 cm; w. 49 cm; thickness 1.5 cm) that represents the holy Virgin Mary seated on a throne, holding the Infant Christ in her lap, flanked by two military saints, St. George – the one without beard – and St. Theodore Stratelates. Behind the Virgin Mary are two angels with scepters looking upwards to the hand of God. The eyes of Mary look away from the beholder. The Christ Child is depicted with a childlike body and a mature head. The faces of the angels show a continuation of Hellenistic tradition.

An icon of the 6th-7th century preserves one of the earliest representations of St. Peter (h. 92.8 cm; w. 53 cm; thickness 1.2 cm). The Apostle is shown in bust form with keys and cross-staff before a niche. Three medallions above represent Jesus in the center, with the Virgin Mary to the right and a youthful saint to the left, probably John the Evangelist. The artist shows a great sense of color harmony and mastery of various brush techniques. Because of the high quality of execution, this icon must have been a Constantinopolitan product.

The Three Hebrews in the Furnace is an Old Testament theme that appears frequently in early Christian art. The three Hebrews stand in frontal pose in a sea of red flames. An angel comforts them; he holds a long staff that is surmounted by a cross, perhaps to indicate that the three Hebrews were rescued by the power of the Cross. This 6th-century icon (h. 35.5 cm; w. 49.6 cm; thickness 1.1 cm) is remarkable for its expressive use of highlights to help the modeling of the figures in the classical tradition.

The Nativity is one of the most popular subjects of early Christian art. In a plaque (center of triptych: h. 32.5 cm; w. 19.7 cm) the Infant Christ is depicted lying on the manger. The Holy Virgin lies on a beige mattress decorated with rosettes. Joseph sits on a wooden stool in the lower right corner. The scene is conflated with the Bathing of the Child on the lower part and the Adoration of the Shepherds to the left of the manger. Stylistically the icon has the characters of the Palestinian school of painting and can be assigned to the 8th-9th century.

The influence of the liturgy and ritual increased dramatically in the Byzantine church in the 10th and 11th centuries. The cult of the bishop-saints grew in importance with the renewal of the liturgy after 843. Bishop Nicholas, whose following was clearly established in the East from the 6th century, became widely known.

In one of the icons (h. 43 cm; w. 33.1 cm; thickness 2.4 cm) the bust-like figure of Nicholas is represented. He wears the bishop's vestments and holds a jewel-studded codex in his left hand, while his right hand is held before his breast. The gold frame is occupied by 10 medallions: at the top is Christ between Peter and Paul. At the sides are four soldier-saints. The watching upper pair are, at the left, St. Demetrius, and at the right, St. George. The lower pair are St. Theodore and St. Procopius. At the bottom are the three physician saints, Cosmas and Damian and Panteleimon. This is probably the earliest icon with medallions decorating the frame. Its artistic quality suggests that it was painted by a great artist of Constantinople at the end of the 10th century.

The icon of the Heavenly Ladder (h. 41 cm; w. 29.5 cm; thickness 1.8 cm) shows a ladder of 30 rungs representing the 30 virtues that the monks must acquire. Temptations cause many people to fall, or the devils pull them from the ladder. But John Climacus himself reaches heaven first, followed by Antonius, the first bishop of Sinai. John Climacus was the famous author and abbot of St. Catherine's. The icon can be dated to the first half of the 12th century.

One of the most interesting icons is that of Moses before the Burning Bush (h. 92 cm; w. 64 cm; thickness 3 cm). This subject is very popular in Sinai; Moses was highly revered by Jewish, Christian and Muslim pilgrims. Moses is depicted as he removes his shoes. His face reflects vitality, forcefulness and innocence. In the upper-right corner there is a very faint Greek inscription that gives the verse from Exodus 3:4 (*God called unto him out of the midst of the bush and said Moses, Moses. And he said, Here am I*). The sensitive treatment of the landscape and plastic quality of the figure points to a competent artist of the 12th-13th century.

The belief in the transference of the relics of St. Catherine to Sinai are responsible for the great fame of the Sinai monastery. Therefore it is not surprising that many of the icons depict her with scenes of her life and martyrdom. In one of the earliest icons (h. 75 cm; w. 51 cm; thickness 2.2 cm) of St. Catherine (12th-13th century), she is represented frontally in imperial garments to underline her royal origin. The border is decorated with 12 scenes, most of which emphasize her persistence in the Christian faith and her martyrdom. A 17th-century icon shows St. Catherine with the books representing her learning, and the wheel of her martyrdom. The monastery is pictured at her feet. Six scenes from the life of St. Catherine are depicted on her sides; top left and right she is looking at the Christ Child on the lap of the Holy Virgin Mary; to the left she is speaking to the emperor, and below she is teaching the empress. To the right, St. Catherine is beheaded; and below, her holy remains are transported by two angels to Mount Catherine. A small, early 18th-century icon (h. 28.6 cm; w. 39 cm) shows the monastery with its walls in the lower-left part; the main church with the apparition of the Burning Bush. The mosque with minaret and the monks' cells are depicted. The reception of the bishop by the monks of the monastery is also shown. In the background, at the top left, Moses is shown receiving the Law; to the right is the entombment of the relics of St. Catherine by two angels. Different chapels in the foothills are pictured.

The Flight of the Holy Family into Egypt

The Gospel of Matthew refers to the Flight of the Holy Family into

Above:
The Nativity of Christ, *8th-9th century. Center of a triptych. Tempera on panel, 32.5 x 19.7 cm.*

Opposite page:
St. Catherine surrounded by scenes of her life and martyrdom, *early 13th century. Tempera on panel, 75 x 51 cm.*

Following pages:
Iacovos Moskos, The Life of St. Catherine, *first quarter of the 18th century. Tempera on panel, 28.6 x 39 cm.*

Η ΑΓΙΑ
ΕΚΑΤΕΡΝΑ

ΙΕΟΝ
ὈΡΩϹ ϹΗΝΑ
507

Opposite page:
A leaf from the Codex Sinaiticus, *4th century .*
Much of the Codex, which contains the Old and New Testaments, the "Epistle of Barnabas" and part of the "Shepherd of Hermas," was allowed to leave the monastery in the 19th century and was purchased from the government of the U.S.S.R. in 1933 by the British Museum for 100,000 English pounds. A dozen leaves remain in the monastery.

Following pages:
Codex Syriacus, *5th century.*
More than 4,000 manuscripts, three quarters of them in Greek, are preserved in the monastery. This document, containing parts of the New Testament, is the most important.

Egypt with the following words:

...behold, the angel of the Lord appeareth to Joseph in a dream, saying, Arise, and take the young child and his mother, and flee into Egypt, and be thou there until I bring thee word: for Herod will seek the young child to destroy him. When he arose, he took the young child and his mother by night, and departed into Egypt: And was there until the death of Herod: that it might be fulfilled which was spoken of the Lord by the prophet, saying, Out of Egypt have I called my son. (Matt. 2:13-15).

The Coptic Church commemorates the Flight of the Holy Family into Egypt on the 24th of the Coptic month Bachons, corresponding to the 1st of June. This great event continued to appeal to the imagination of later preachers; many fascinating details of the sojourn of the Holy Family in Egypt are mentioned in Coptic, Armenian, Ethiopian and Arabic writings. Many sites in the Delta and Middle Egypt boast of a tradition of the Holy Family having visited or rested there.

In Sinai, there are some traditional sites associated with the Flight into Egypt. The Holy Family crossed the Sinai Peninsula by the northern caravan route, alongside the Mediterranean littoral, from Gaza to Raphia. This city was the seat of a bishop during the Byzantine period. The first town that the Holy Family reached after Raphia was Rhinokorua (El-Arish), where the Romans exiled criminals and cut off their noses. From there the Holy Family went to Ostracine at the eastern extremity of Lake Berdawil; some identify it with the village called Khirbat el-Flusiya, others with the hamlet of Zananiq. The last station of the Holy Family in Sinai was the important city Pelusium before crossing the Isthmus of Suez south of Lake Manzalah.

Reverence for the Holy Family is widespread in Egypt, and the Copts take pride in that great event.

Other Churches

On the summit of Gebel Musa is situated a small and simple chapel. According to tradition, the chapel is built on the site where Moses received the Law. Around 560, Antonius of Placenta visited the church before its enlargement in the time of Justinian. A new building was constructed over it in 1934, which encloses roughly half of the central aisle of the Justinian church. The church is decorated with many beautiful icons.

The oasis of Pharan (Fayran), "Pearl of Sinai," was the center of anchorite life of the Egyptian type. When Antonius of Placenta passed through, he was saluted in Egyptian. Macarius is mentioned as a bishop of Pharan in a letter of Emperor Macrian. During the 5th century the hermitages of Pharan suffered from the raids of the Blemmyes, a Nubian tribe, and the Bedouin of the desert. It would seem that the bishopric of Pharan disappeared in the 7th century, to the advantage of the Monastery of St. Catherine. The Cathedral of Pharan was once an imposing one. Its remains can still be seen there; some of its Byzantine capitals are decorated with crosses. It belongs to the 6th century. Recently, excavations were carried out on the site of Pharan and in the ruins on the neighboring mountains. The ruins of the town church were investigated; it was erected in the 5th century. At Gebel Tahuna the remains of two churches were cleaned and examined; one belongs to the 6th century and the other, at the top of the mountain, dates to the 4th century. The latter is perhaps the same church

ΟΝ ΚΥ ΚΑΙ Ε[illegible]
ΑΥΤΟΥΣ ΚΣ ΕΝ ΧΕ[illegible]
ΑΙΝ ΜΕΙ[illegible]
ΙΣΧΥΣΕΝ ΧΕΙΡ ΜΑ[illegible]
ΑΜ ΕΠΙ ΙΣΛ ΚΑΙ Ε
ΠΟΙΗΣΑΝ ΕΑΥΤΟΙΣ
ΟΙ ΥΙΟΙ [illegible]
ΣΩΠΟΥ ΜΑΔΙΑΜ
ΤΑΣ ΤΡΥΜΑΛΙΑΣ ΤΑΣ
ΕΝ ΤΟΙΣ ΟΡΕΣΙΝ ΚΑΙ
ΤΑΣ ΣΠΗΛΑΙΑ ΚΑΙ ΤΑ
ΚΡΕΜΑΣΤΑ ΚΑΙ ΕΓΕ
ΝΕΤΟ ΕΑΝ ΕΣΠΕΙ
ΡΟΝ ΟΙ ΥΙΟΙ ΙΣΛ ΚΑΙ
ΑΝΕΒΑΙΝΑΝ ΜΑΔΙ
ΑΜ ΚΑΙ ΑΜΑΛΗΚ ΚΑΙ
ΟΙ ΑΝΑΤΟΛΩΝ ΣΥ
ΝΑΝΕΒΑΙΝΟΝ ΑΥ
ΤΟΙΣ ΚΑΙ ΠΑΡΕΝΕ
ΒΑΛΛΟΝ ΕΙΣ ΑΥΤΟΥΣ
ΚΑΙ ΚΑΤΕΦΘΕΙΡΑΝ
ΤΟΥΣ ΚΑΡΠΟΥΣ ΑΥΤ
ΕΙΣ ΓΑΖΑΝ ΚΑΙ ΟΥ
ΚΑΤΕΛΙΠΟΝ ΥΠΟΣΤΑ
ΣΙΝ ΖΩΗΣ ΕΝ ΤΗ ΓΗ
ΙΣΛ ΟΥΔΕ ΕΝ ΤΟΙΣ
ΠΟΙΜΝΙΟΙΣ ΤΑΥΡΟΝ
ΚΑΙ ΟΝΟΝ ΟΤΙ ΑΥΤΟΙ
ΚΑΙ ΑΙ ΚΤΗΣΕΙΣ ΑΥΤΩΝ
ΑΝΕΒΑΙΝΟΝ ΚΑΙ ΑΙ
ΣΚΗΝΑΙ ΑΥΤΩΝ
ΙΖ ΠΑΡΕΓΕΙΝΟΝΤΟ ΚΑ
ΘΩΣ ΑΚΡΙΣ ΕΙΣ ΠΛΗ
ΘΟΣ ΚΑΙ ΑΥΤΟΙΣ ΚΑΙ
ΤΟΙΣ ΚΑΜΗΛΟΙΣ ΑΥ
ΤΩΝ ΟΥΚ ΗΝ ΑΡΙΘΜΟΣ
ΚΑΙ ΗΡΧΟΝΤΟ ΕΙΣ ΤΗΝ
ΓΗΝ ΙΣΛ ΚΑΙ ΔΙΕΦΘΕΙ
ΡΟΝ ΑΥΤΗΝ ΚΑΙ Ε
ΠΤΩΧΕΥΣΕΝ ΙΣΛ
ΣΦΟΔΡΑ ΑΠΟ ΠΡΟΣΩ
ΠΟΥ ΜΑΔΙΑΜ ΚΑΙ Ε
ΒΟΗΣΑΝ ΥΙΟΙ ΙΣΛ
ΠΡΟΣ ΚΝ ΑΠΟ ΠΡΟ
ΣΩΠΟΥ ΜΑΔΙΑΜ ΚΑΙ
ΕΞΑΠΕΣΤΙΛΕΝ ΚΣ
ΑΝΔΡΑ ΠΡΟΦΗΤΗΝ
ΠΡΟΣ ΤΟΥΣ ΥΙΟΥΣ ΙΣΛ

ΚΑΙ ΕΙΠΕΝ ΑΥΤΟΙΣ
ΤΑΔΕ ΛΕΓΕΙ ΚΣ Ο ΘΣ ΙΣΛ
ΕΓΩ ΕΙΜΙ Ο ΑΝΑΓΑ
ΓΩΝ ΥΜΑΣ ΕΚ ΓΗΣ
ΑΙΓΥΠΤΟΥ ΚΑΙ ΕΚ
ΧΕΙΡΟΣ ΠΑΝΤΩΝ ΤΩΝ
[illegible]ΚΟΝΤΩΝ ΥΜΑΣ
ΚΑΙ ΕΞΕΒΑΛΟΝ ΑΥΤΟΥΣ
ΕΚ ΠΡΟΣΩΠΟΥ ΥΜΩΝ
ΚΑΙ ΕΔΩΚΑ ΥΜΙΝ
ΤΗΝ ΓΗΝ ΑΥΤΩΝ
ΚΑΙ ΕΙΠΑ ΥΜΙΝ ΕΓΩ
ΚΣ Ο ΘΣ ΥΜΩΝ ΟΥ
ΦΟΒΗΘΗΣΕΣΘΕ
ΤΟΥΣ ΘΕΟΥΣ ΤΟΥ Α
ΜΟΡΡΑΙΟΥ ΕΝ ΟΙΣ
ΥΜΕΙΣ ΚΑΘΗΣΕΣΘΕ
ΕΝ ΤΗ ΓΗ ΑΥΤΩΝ
ΚΑΙ ΟΥΚ ΕΙΣΗΚΟΥΣΑ
ΤΕ ΤΗΣ ΦΩΝΗΣ ΜΟΥ
ΚΑΙ ΗΛΘΕΝ ΑΓΓΕΛΟΣ
ΚΥ ΚΑΙ ΕΚΑΘΙΣΕΝ
ΥΠΟ ΤΗΝ ΤΕΡΜΙΝΘΟΝ
ΤΗΝ ΕΝ ΕΦΡΑΘΑ ΤΗΝ
ΤΗΝ ΙΩΑΣ ΠΑΤΡΟΣ ΤΟΥ
ΕΣΔΡΙ
ΚΑΙ ΓΕΔΕΩΝ ΥΙΟΣ ΑΥ
ΤΟΥ ΡΑΒΔΙΖΩΝ ΣΕΙ
ΤΟΝ ΕΝ ΛΗΝΩ ΕΙΣ ΕΚ
ΦΥΓΕΙΝ ΑΠΟ ΠΡΟΣΩ
ΠΟΥ ΤΟΥ ΜΑΔΙΑΜ
ΚΑΙ ΩΦΘΗ ΑΥΤΩ
ΑΓΓΕΛΟΣ ΚΥ ΚΑΙ ΕΙ
ΠΕΝ ΠΡΟΣ ΑΥΤΟΝ
ΚΣ ΜΕΤΑ ΣΟΥ ΙΣΧΥ
ΡΟΣ ΤΩΝ ΔΥΝΑΜΕΩΝ
ΚΑΙ ΕΙΠΕΝ ΠΡΟΣ ΑΥΤΟΝ
ΓΕΔΕΩΝ ΕΝ ΕΜΟΙ
ΚΕ ΚΕ ΜΟΥ ΚΑΙ ΕΙ ΕΣΤΙ
ΚΣ ΜΕΘ ΗΜΩΝ ΕΙΣ
ΤΙ ΕΥΡΕΝ ΗΜΑΣ ΠΑ
ΤΑ ΤΑ ΚΑΚΑ ΤΑΥΤΑ ΚΑΙ
ΠΟΥ ΕΣΤΙΝ ΠΑΝΤΑ
ΤΑ ΘΑΥΜΑΣΙΑ ΑΥΤΟΥ
Α ΔΙΗΓΗΣΑΝΤΟ ΗΜΙ
Ο ΠΑΤΕΡΕΣ ΗΜΩΝ
ΛΕΓΟΝΤΕΣ ΜΗ ΟΥΧΙ
ΕΞ ΑΙΓΥΠΤΟΥ ΑΝΗ

ΓΑΓΕΝ ΗΜΑΣ ΚΣ ΚΑΙ
ΝΥΝ ΕΞΕΡΡΙΨΕΝ ΗΜΑΣ
ΚΣ ΚΑΙ ΕΔΩΚΕΝ
ΗΜΑΣ ΕΝ ΧΕΙΡΙ ΜΑ
ΔΙΑΜ ΚΑΙ ΑΠΕΣΤΡΑ
ΦΕΝ ΠΡΟΣ ΑΥΤΟΝ ΑΓ
ΓΕΛΟΣ ΚΥ ΚΑΙ ΕΙΠΕΝ
ΠΟΡΕΥΟΥ ΕΝ ΙΣΧΥΙ
ΣΟΥ ΤΑΥΤΗ ΚΑΙ ΣΩ
ΣΕΙΣ ΤΟΝ ΙΣΛ ΕΚ ΧΕΙ
ΡΟΣ ΜΑΔΙΑΜ ΙΔΟΥ Ε
ΞΑΠΕΣΤΙΛΑ ΣΕ ΚΑΙ
ΕΙΠΕΝ ΠΡΟΣ ΑΥΤΟΝ
ΓΕΔΕΩΝ ΕΝ ΕΜΟΙ
ΚΕ ΜΟΥ ΕΝ ΤΙΝΙ ΣΩ
ΣΩ ΤΟΝ ΙΣΛ ΙΔΟΥ Η
ΧΙΛΙΑΣ ΜΟΥ ΗΣΘΕ
ΝΗΣΕΝ ΕΝ ΜΑΝΑΣ
ΣΗ ΚΑΙ ΕΓΩ ΕΙΜΙ Ο
ΜΙΚΡΟΤΕΡΟΣ ΕΝ ΟΙ
ΚΩ ΠΑΤΡΟΣ ΜΟΥ
ΚΑΙ ΕΙΠΕΝ ΠΡΟΣ ΑΥ
ΤΟΝ Ο ΑΓΓΕΛΟΣ ΚΥ ΚΣ
ΕΣΤΑΙ ΜΕΤΑ ΣΟΥ ΚΑΙ
ΠΑΤΑΞΕΙΣ ΤΗΝ ΜΑ
ΔΙΑΜ ΩΣΕΙ ΑΝΔΡΑ
ΕΝΑ
ΚΑΙ ΕΙΠΕΝ ΠΡΟΣ ΑΥ
ΤΟΝ ΓΕΔΕΩΝ ΙΔΕ ΕΙ
ΕΥΡΟΝ ΕΛΕΟΣ ΕΝ ΟΦ
ΘΑΛΜΟΙΣ ΣΟΥ ΚΑΙ
ΠΟΙΗΣΕΙΣ ΕΜΟΙ ΣΗ
ΜΕΡΟΝ ΠΑΝ ΟΤΙ ΣΥ
ΛΑΛΗΣ ΜΕΤ ΕΜΟΥ
ΜΗ ΧΩΡΙΣΘΗΣ ΕΝ
ΤΕΥΘΕΝ ΕΩΣ ΤΟΥ Ε
ΛΘΕΙΝ ΜΕ ΠΡΟΣ ΣΕ ΚΑΙ
ΕΞΟΙΣΩ ΤΗΝ ΘΥΣΙΑ
ΚΑΙ ΘΗΣΩ ΕΝΩΠΙ
ΟΝ ΣΟΥ ΚΑΙ ΕΙΠΕΝ
ΕΓΩ ΕΙΜΙ ΚΑΘΗΣΟΜΑΙ
ΕΩΣ ΤΟΥ ΕΠΙΣΤΡΕ
ΨΑΙ ΣΕ ΚΑΙ ΓΕΔΕΩΝ
ΕΙΣΗΛΘΕΝ ΚΑΙ ΕΠΟΙ
ΗΣΕΝ ΕΡΙΦΟΝ ΑΙ
ΓΩΝ ΚΑΙ ΟΙΦΙ ΑΛΕΥ
ΡΟΥ ΑΖΥΜΑ ΚΑΙ ΤΑ
ΚΡΕΑ ΕΘΗΚΕΝ ΕΝ
ΕΠΙ ΤΟ ΚΑΝΟΥΝ

ΑΥΤΟ ΚΟΦΙΝΩ ΚΑΙ ΤΟ
ΖΩΜΟΝ ΕΝΕΒΑΛΕΝ
ΕΝ ΤΗ ΧΥΤΡΑ ΚΑΙ Ε
ΞΗΝΕΓΚΕΝ ΑΥΤΑ ΠΡΟΣ
ΑΥΤΟΝ ΥΠΟ ΤΗΝ ΤΕΡΕ
ΜΙΝΘΟΝ ΚΑΙ ΠΡΟΣ
ΗΓΓΙΣΕΝ ΚΑΙ ΕΙΠΕΝ
ΠΡΟΣ ΑΥΤΟΝ Ο ΑΓΓΕ
ΛΟΣ ΤΟΥ ΘΥ ΛΑΒΕ ΤΑ
ΚΡΕΑ ΚΑΙ ΤΑ ΑΖΥΜΑ
ΚΑΙ ΘΕΣ ΠΡΟΣ ΤΗΝ
ΠΕΤΡΑΝ ΕΚΕΙΝΗΝ
ΚΑΙ ΤΟΝ ΖΩΜΟΝ
ΕΧΟΜΕΝΑ ΕΚΧΕΟΝ
ΚΑΙ ΕΠΟΙΗΣΕΝ ΟΥ
ΤΩΣ
ΚΑΙ ΕΞΕΤΙΝΕΝ Ο ΑΓ
ΓΕΛΟΣ ΚΥ ΤΟ ΑΚΡΟΝ
ΤΗΣ ΡΑΒΔΟΥ ΤΗΣ ΕΝ
ΤΗ ΧΕΙΡΙ ΑΥΤΟΥ ΚΑΙ
ΗΨΑΤΟ ΤΩΝ ΚΡΕΩΝ
ΚΑΙ ΤΩΝ ΑΖΥΜΩΝ
ΚΑΙ ΑΝΕΒΗ ΠΥΡ ΕΚ
ΤΗΣ ΠΕΤΡΑΣ ΚΑΙ ΚΑ
ΤΕΦΑΓΕΝ ΤΑ ΚΡΕΑ
ΚΑΙ ΤΟΥΣ ΑΖΥΜΟΥΣ
ΚΑΙ Ο ΑΓΓΕΛΟΣ ΚΥ
ΟΥΤΟΣ ΕΣΤΙΝ ΚΑΙ
ΕΙΠΕΝ ΓΕΔΕΩΝ Α Α
ΚΕ ΜΟΥ ΚΕ ΟΤΙ ΕΙΔΟΝ
ΑΓΓΕΛΟΝ ΚΥ ΠΡΟ
ΣΩΠΟΝ ΠΡΟΣ ΠΡΟ
ΣΩΠΟΝ
ΚΑΙ ΕΙΠΕΝ ΑΥΤΩ ΚΣ
ΕΙΡΗΝΗ ΣΟΙ ΜΗ ΦΟ
ΒΟΥ ΜΗ ΑΠΟΘΑ
ΝΗΣ ΚΑΙ ΩΚΟΔΟ
ΜΗΣΕΝ ΕΚΕΙ ΓΕΔΕ
ΩΝ ΘΥΣΙΑΣΤΗΡΙ
ΤΩ ΚΩ ΚΑΙ ΕΠΕΚΑ
ΛΕΣΕΝ ΑΥΤΟ ΕΙΡΗ
ΝΗ ΚΥ ΕΩΣ ΤΗΣ Η
ΜΕΡΑΣ ΤΑΥΤΗΣ ΕΤΙ
ΑΥΤΟΥ ΟΝΤΟΣ ΕΝ Ε
ΦΡΑΘΑ ΠΑΤΡΟΣ ΤΟΥ
ΕΣΔΡΙ
ΙΓ ΚΑΙ ΕΓΕΝΕΤΟ ΕΝ ΤΗ
ΝΥΚΤΙ ΕΚΕΙΝΗ ΚΑΙ

[illegible] ΦΑΛΛΩΝ [illegible]
ΓΕΔΕΩΝ ΟΤΙ ΑΓΓΕΛΟΣ ΚΥ

described by Aetheria at the end of the 4th century at the very spot on the mountain: "The very lofty steep mountain which overhangs Pharan is the place where Moses prayed, Joshua defeated Amalek; a church has now been built at the spot where Moses prayed..."

Raithou (El-Tor) is the site of the martyrdom of the 40 monks who were massacred, perhaps in the 4th or 5th century, by the Blemmyes. The Egyptian monk Ammonius of Canopus near Alexandria describes a semi-anchoritism at Raithou very similar to that of Egypt. It would seem that the relics of the castle with its church at Raithou are from the time of Emperor Justinian.

The historian Abu el-Makarim (13th century) writes that in his time there were numerous churches and monasteries in ruins in Pelusium. During recent excavations the remains of a basilica and a martyrium – a chapel built in honor of a martyr – were discovered. The bronze coins found there came from the second half of the 4th century to the first half of the 6th century. Pelusium became an important center of monasticism, and the best-known of the monks from that region was Isidorus (about 355-435), who was a theologian.

Khirbat el-Flusiya is situated at the eastern extremity of Lake Berdawil. It was a harbor of commercial significance, because its position was close to the most important military caravan route linking Egypt and Palestine from Pelusium via Rhinokorua to Gaza. The remains of a fortress-monastery and two churches of basilican type were discovered there. They may belong to the 6th century.

Mosques

Sinai is mentioned in the Koran as Tur Sinin (XCV, 2); the Arab geographers refer to it as Tur Sinai. The caravans of the pilgrims traveled across Sinai carrying the Mehmel on their way to Mecca.

In Wadi el-Shaikh, not far from the Monastery of St. Catherine, lies the tomb of el-Nabi Saleh; his white-domed shrine stands on a small hill. El-Nabi Saleh is venerated by the Bedouin of Sinai and is considered as one of the most honored Muslim saints. Many of the inhabitants of Sinai take part in his annual celebration. On the summit of Gebel Musa is a small mosque, which is highly revered by the Bedouin. Following the annual celebration (*Mulid*) of el-Nabi Saleh, they sacrifice sheep on ruins of the mosque. El-Idrisi, the famous Arab geographer (12th century), mentioned this mosque.

Near the belfry of the Monastery of St. Catherine stands a mosque that was originally a guest house; its minaret faces the church. The mosque measures 10 meters by seven meters; the minaret is nearly 10 meters high. According to tradition, it was built during the reign of the Fatimid Caliph el-Hakim (996-1021). When he approached the monastery, the monks went to meet him. El-Hakim granted them his protection and asked them to build a mosque within the walls of the monastery. The mosque boasts a very valuable rare pulpit (*minbar*). It bears a Kufic text that records that it was a gift of Abu Ali el-Mansur Anushtakin el Amiri in the month Rabi I of the Hegira year 500 (A.D. 1106).

Opposite page:
The minaret and the mosque, erected inside the Monastery of St. Catherine's walls in the early 11th century, stand next to the bell tower.

The Bedouin of Sinai

by Samir Sobhi

In the Bedouin society of Sinai, camels are part of the family. They have a role in customs, traditions and even legislation.

They are both a means of transportation and a source of food, milk and clothing. Known as the "ship of the desert," the camel or *hagan* is the hero of the *hagan* race, running at a speed of 60 kilometers per hour, with its legs almost invisible as it speeds along, provided it is in full health and physical fitness.

It is through camels that the wealth of tribes is measured: they are currency; they are used as brides' dowries and as a means of resolving conflicts between tribes. Compensation paid is in camels, according to the kind of crime committed and the size of the fine.

There is a camel judge, called the *zayady*, whose name comes from his tribe, and who decides matters of camel thefts. Another tribesman, called the *massook*, is an expert in camels and their teeth, and handles all fines.

It is for all these reasons that a Bedouin's wealth is judged in camels. Tradition enforces a respect for camel ownership, and hence serious punishment for camel thieves. Sometimes a thief or his tribe must pay a fine calculated according to every footstep in the distance between the place of theft and the place where the camel was taken.

For centuries, camels have been the main source of transportation for the Bedouin. But modern times are bringing change. With the increase in dependence upon modern means of transportation, and the asphalting of highways to link the different parts of Sinai, there has been a corresponding decrease in the importance of the camel's role. This has led to a lack of interest in raising, training, and disciplining camels. There are now large numbers of free-roaming camels, grazing in the desert for long months without their owners.

Kamelos is a Greek word, derived from the Phoenician and Hebrew *Gamal*. In Ibn Al Manzoor's dictionary, *Lessan Al Arab*, the camel is a lion, and it holds the same status as a boy or a slave. There are basically two kinds of camels: the single-humped Arabian camel and the two-humped Bactrian camel. These are the biggest of the camel family, whose members include the vicuna, the llama, the guanaco and the alpaca.

Camels in Sinai are relatively small in size, having a light yellowish color, and are suitable for riding. Their life span is 30 to 40 years, which makes Arabs believe and say that they are one of God's gifts. Although they are slow to breed, delivering their first calf at the age of five, then once every two years, their productive period is very long, lasting for as long as 40 years.

A camel is capable of enduring exhaustion, and is called the "ship

Opposite page:
Two Bedouin women collect dates along the Mediterranean beach at Sheikh Zouaid.

of the desert" precisely because it is more able than a donkey to survive, easier to lead, and better at carrying heavy burdens. Its underfoot is flat and even-toed, in order to sink into the sand with stability.

Its stomach is a hollow, divided into rooms or bladders that are filled with water whenever the camel drinks. The drinking process itself lasts 15 minutes, while the water lasts from 20 to 30 days inside its body. Its food consists of tree branches, thorns and grass; and its eyes have the ability to see well during day or night.

The camel provides wealth for the Bedouin: its meat and its milk give food; its hair becomes cloth; its skin is used to make shoes, belts, gloves and water bottles. Even its tail is used as fuel. Its milk production ranges between 1,600 to 2,000 kilograms over a period of 15 months.

The Tribal Movement

When the Byzantine Empire gave some Arabs the task of protecting its borders, a great movement of tribes began. The most famous of these tribes were the Ghasasna, the Lahm and the Gezam, the latter two of the Kahlan family. The influence and sovereignty of these tribes extended from Oman to the borders of Sharkeya governorate in the Nile Valley. They were basically Christians, until Arab Muslims found their way to Egypt under Amr Ibn El-As.

With the Islamic conquest, Sinai no longer was a target in itself for these migrating tribes. In the villages of Egypt they found what is lacking in Sinai: abundant riches and resources. From that time onwards, Sinai became a mere passageway for Arab tribes migrating to Egypt.

The Bedouin invented a tattoo to identify the ownership of animals, because pasture lands extend over large areas where camels and cattle are left to graze unattended. They might remain for long periods of time away from their owners. Bedouins therefore tattoo the animals with different signs and shapes, proving the ownership of each tribe. These are called *halal* animals.

Bedouin sew wool feeding-bags for their camels, and the saddle is known as the *watar* or *haweya*. The saddle is also known as the *ghabeet* or *shaddad*. It has two hair belts, and they go round the front of the stomach and back to its posterior.

Bedouin also sing for their camels. They drink and walk because they enjoy drinking and walking to the sound of the *heda'a*, which is the camel's song. Every tribe has its own special tunes and lyrics in the *heda'a* that distinguish them from each other. A tribe like the Teeh sing the *heda'a* to their camels while they are giving them water at the palm wells. They also sing while sitting on the backs of camels, calling those songs the *mawaleya*. The *heda'a* is believed to have great influence over camels.

It is said that a prince passed an Arab sheikh and saw a slave in iron shackles. The prince asked curiously: "What did this slave do to deserve such punishment?" The sheikh answered: "Follow me." He took the prince to the stables where exhausted camels lay resting. He turned to the slave and ordered: "Sing."

He sang, and the camels jumped excitedly to their feet, as though nothing was wrong with them. The sheikh explained: "This slave drove these camels a long distance, carrying heavy burdens and loads, singing to them until they increased their speed and reached this state of exhaustion...!"

Whenever Bedouin wish to invade and fight, they ride the *hagan*. They run until they are close to their target, then leave their camels and lie low to the ground. Some men remain behind to protect them. They then go forward in one row, and upon seeing the enemy begin shooting. Once their ammunition is finished, they fight with their swords and do not return except victorious or vanquished.

In the fighting arenas, their knights cry out their sisters' names or their daughters', saying: "I am the brother of so and so, or the father of so and so." And then they shout: "Slaughter, slaughter!"

Huge celebrations are arranged for marriages, in which the entire tribe comes out to participate. In the morning, a huge *hagan* race among the men is organized, while in the evening, folk music begins, together with singing and dancing. Camels also dance, sometimes alone and sometimes with rider.

On the wedding day, the bride's father asks the groom a traditional question three times: "Do you accept marrying my daughter?" The groom answers "yes" three times in front of witnesses. The bride's father then gives the groom a small piece of wood, known as the *kasla*, which is basically a part of a tree branch known as the *rhythm*, and he tells the groom: "You have engaged my daughter, and she is now your responsibility." When the groom takes the *kasla* he tells the father: "I accept her as my wife, by God's *Sunna* and the Prophet." The *fatha* is then read from the Holy Koran.

A tent called the *barza* is prepared for the groom. His bride enters into it with her closest relative. The rest of the women remain outside with the men. The groom's relatives start slaughtering cattle for the guests at the door of the *barza*. They play and entertain, then the groom's relatives give presents in the shape of cattle, wheat and money, as a wedding shower. This is considered a debt that should be repaid later.

The groom stays with his bride in the *barza* from one to three days. Custom dictates that the bride escapes from the *barza* before the third day, and the husband follows her to live with her in the wilderness, away from the tents of his family, for a period between one week to one month. During that time his family sends him food, until another tent is prepared for them near their tents. This is his new home, and they sing special wedding songs to the bride.

Generally speaking, the Bedouin man is always careful about providing a suitable marital life, ensuring its continuation and fully carrying the family's responsibilities. There is a close, mutual-respect relationship between a man and his wife, with each partner preserving the other's rights. Marriage is a word of honor, and there are no documents or contracts, although the local governorates recently have begun requesting marital registrations.

Although the advent of private homes has spread to some places in the north of Sinai, and many Bedouin live in homes built of stone and bricks, some still live in tents made of camel hair, built in the shape of a bull, with its door facing the east. The tent usually has nine pillars, three in the middle, and three on each side. It is divided into two sections: one for the women and one for the men. Living in tents, however, is confined to winter and spring, in order to avoid the cold and the rain. In summer, huts made of branches and straw help avoid the heat and winds. These are called the *araesh*, from which the name El-Arish is derived.

Among several items in the home are: *al monsef*, which is a round, wide plate made of wood for

Above:
An El-Arish Bedouin and his camel.

Following pages:
A mother camel and her baby, at Dahab.

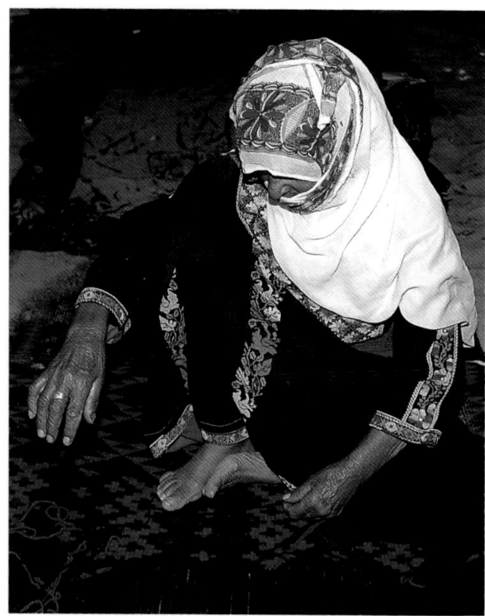

Above:
An elderly Bedouin woman weaves the traditional decorated fabric in El-Arish.

Opposite page:
Bedouin women are famous for their tattoos.

serving food; a *bateya* which is a smaller plate for the head of the family's use; the *karmeya* or *zalfaa*, which is smaller than both, used to bake flour and present food to guests; the *henaya* is yet smaller and deeper than all the rest. There is a *kadah*, which is a square vessel made of wood, having a handle and a tip, and is used for milking camels and for drinking water. In addition to these, there is a stone mill used for milling flour, and a sieve for straining seeds. There are large iron sheets for bread, and aluminum pots and pans, which they buy without their covers. A coffee set consists of a large teapot made of copper, and a roaster.

One of the most important pieces of furniture is the *kharag*. It is used during traveling, and is made of white or colored wool, on which is sewn some shredded fiber. There is the *mezwad*, which looks like the *kharag* and is also made in the same manner, used also in traveling to carry flour. The *kerba* is a famous water vessel made of sheep skin. In the east of El-Arish, they use vessels made of pottery instead of the *kerba*. There are also the *magareb*, which are sacks for tobacco made of deer skin or cattle skin. The *fallayeen* is used to smoke the tobacco, and is usually made of tree branches. Its fuel or flint stone is extracted from dense mountains near Yalek Mountain, or Orf Mountain in the east of Aqaba.

The diet of the Sinai Bedouin consists of wheat, barley, corn, rice, lentils, dates, fish, and meat. Seeds are ground in mills and kneaded in the *bateya*, then baked into bread on sheets or as round, flat loafs on stone to be used while traveling. This is called the *mallah*.

There are many unique dishes. *Greesha* is wheat ground in the stone mill until it becomes harshly granulated, then heated well and poured onto a plate, covering it with mild fat or oil. *Aseeda* is made by boiling water in a pan and gradually pouring flour over it, stirring until it thickens. It is then poured onto a plate and eaten. Sometimes boiled milk is used instead of water and this is called the *telbana*. *Matbookha* is bread boiled in milk and in hot fat. *Dafeena* is bread or boiled rice in meat bouillon. The *dakka* is basically weeds that grow in the desert. Branches of the different plants are used, such as the zachum tree, wormwood, watercress, prunes and thyme. They dry it, grind it and mix it, then dip the *mallah* bread in it and eat it. Lamb meat is sometimes cooked in a stone oven in the shape of a small hut with a door. Firewood placed inside is heated red hot. They then slaughter a lamb or a goat, skin it and open its belly. After cleaning it, they wrap it and place it in the stone hut. They scatter embers over it, close the door and leave it for over an hour. It is truly a delicious grill.

A woman does not eat with her husband at the same table, out of courtesy to him, and she does not call him by his name, but rather by his elder son's or daughter's name, or by his father's name. A woman also swears by her father's head and not by her husband's head, nor by her son's arm.

The Bedouin women are characterized by grace, light movement, intelligent eyes, dark colors and the sparsity of the hair on their cheeks. Bedouin women are also famous for their tattoos, especially lip tattoos. They are famous for hospitality, honoring camels, helping others, taking revenge, caring for neighbors, feeling gratitude, respecting honor, keeping the oath, pride of ancestery, courage, hating to be tied to a certain system, demanding their rights, and possessing a love of equality and freedom.

Bedouin clothing is loose and

comfortable. A man wears a shirt beneath another long shirt made of raw material. This is called *abu kerdan*, meaning a bird. It was thus called because of the length of its sleeves. Should the wearer throw his hands to his sides, the shirt would almost touch the floor. They might wear over it a *kabr*, which is like a caftan, and on top of all that a black cloak called *dafya*. In winter, the *ge'dan*, made of untanned lamb skin, is worn over the dress upside down, so that its fur would be on the back.

Turbans with *marira* are a headdress made of camel wool, and the Olaykat Bedouins are famous for it. The turban is a white handkerchief, and the *marira* is a headband made of lamb's wool or camel's wool. One might wear over the turban a colored silk shawl or a white wool shawl, tying both with the *marira*.

The women wear *abu kerdan* that they buy dyed in blue. They are then darkened with a paint made from plant roots, combined with white and black hair, and tied round their waists three times. They might wear over it a red belt called the *saghifa*, from which shredded fiber comes out on the right side all the way down to the knee.

The veil is heavy, covering the entire face, with only the eyes showing. It consists of the *weka*, which is a piece of black cotton cloth with colored silk threads covering the ears and head. The veil is tied with two strings beneath the chin. The veil is also a piece of red, yellow or white shredded fiber, sown with silk threads, and small pieces of gold, silver or copper, lined in a row on both sides or on its lower edge. It covers the head from the nose to beneath the chin, and might reach the belt.

On the forehead, there is a piece of material made of the same fabric as the veil, covering the entire forehead. It has two rings on each side, dangling on the sides of the forehead and shoulders. There are also strings of old currency, called *shakka*, tied with ribbons dangling down, tieing them to the veil, and a ribbon going backwards and tied to the back of the head, thus holding the veil and the *weka* together. From the middle of the forehead another ribbon dangles over to the nose, pulling the veil from the middle.

The *Borko* is a headdress that the Sinai woman decorates with care. It is closer to a symbol than a mere piece of clothing, and its colors and decorations reveal social status and marital status. At the same time, the *Borko* is a symbol of the tribe, people or house of those who wear it.

Beads, too, have a special status with Bedouin women. Coins and beads are sewn on the *khemar*, or waistcoat, the headdress and parts of the dress. The Bedouin man wears rings on two fingers only, the ring finger and the smallest finger, and these are decorated with stones. Sometimes they write their names on the rings and they are used for stamping instead of finger printing.

Bedouin Society

Everyone is in the market. It is the central gathering place for everyone in the area, where the Bedouin exhibits merchandise and art in an expansive manner, showing exactly what the land and the hands have produced. There is the Thursday market in El-Arish, the Saturday market in Rafah, the Sunday market in Al Sheikh Zoweid, and the Wednesday market in Koseema. This latter is famous for a place called Ein Gadirat; a fountainhead, six kilometers out of town, it is the only fountainhead in Sinai that has abundant water emanating from rocks and flowing into the small valley to irrigate the olive trees.

The market is well organized, exhibiting its products neatly and simply. Bedouin use either cash or barter. One of the most important products is herbal medicine: The *gaabara* is used for indigestion, the *baaithran* for dental pains, and the *hanzal* (colocynth) for constipation. There are beautiful, colorful clothes, full of threads and decorations. Earrings and bracelets are made of silver, shell, amber, and coral; and there are rings of different semiprecious stones of different colors. There are head and chest amulets sewn with colored beads made with great skill, and beautiful old silver coins.

In the market the popular artist works in tattoos, which are the Bedouin women's basic adornment. Tattoos on the forehead are called *halil*, and on the sides of the mouth there is a flower. On the lower lip and down to the chin, there is the *howaifer*; and on the chin there is the *darb*, or an ant's road. On the back of the fingers and the palms up to the wrists and at the elbow, there are scissors and a fish. From the foot to the middle of the leg, there are several diverse paintings, according to each tattoo artist's taste and art.

We also find a doctor in the market. He is the wise man whose basic cure is cautery, which is used for head, stomach and back pains. Boiled onions are used to wash wounds. Patients drink from onion bouillon, in order to prevent rotting of the wound. Myrrh boiled with fat is used as ointment for wounds. Women burn small scorpions in a grind and sprinkle the ashes over their breasts while breast feeding, as inoculation against scorpion bites.

The Bedouin's industry springs out of needs. Women spin wool and are sometimes seen spinning as they walk with wool on their heads and the spinning wheel in their hands. They sew covers and tent necessities, and make clothes from goat hair, lamb's wool and camel hair. The loom or the spinning wheel consists of two pieces of wood slightly raised from the floor. Between them is a wool reel. A woman sits at the end of the reel, and in her hand there is a knife with which she spins. Spinning is very slow. A woman works all day long and makes no more than two meters.

Dyeing is another task performed by women. They dye wool threads used in sewing, in colors such as red, green and yellow, with an extraction from some wild herbs.

A major industry surrounds camels, horses and cattle. Bedouin invest in them and trade with their male offspring. Camels are found in the Teeh and Lehwayat valleys, where every year the Hoyatat traders from Egypt go to buy any surplus available, or the Bedouins might go with that surplus to the Nile Valley and sell them. Camels, horses and cattle that pass through Sinai from Syria, the Hegaz via El-Arish and Nakhl, and most of the traders who come via the Nakhl Way to Suez or Ismailia, are Arabs of the Wagh, Genba, Al Moweilah and Aqaba. Their most important source of living is renting camels to tourists and officials of the government, in addition to fishing, bird and deer hunting, selling camels, coal, turquoise, rush, wood, and pressed dates.

The tribes of Sinai depend in their living upon pastures, agriculture, bird hunting, fishing, following footprints and trade. There are minor and simple skills such as iron mongering, and making daggers, swords and female accessories.

Among all the tribes, the Maseed is famous for hunting eagles, which are ample during the month of September. Other migrating birds flock close to this tribe,

Above:
The decoration and design of the woman's clothing and the handwoven tablecloth she holds tell she is from North Sinai.

Following pages:
A traditional mural of palm branches decorates this modern-day Bedouin house, appearing as real as the live palm branches at either side.

Opposite page:
"El-Hagan," the annual camel race that attracts competitors from all tribes of Sinai, is held in El-Arish.

especially quail, which is the primary food for eagles. The Maseed sell eagles at very high prices–at times as much as E£10,000 per eagle, or about US$3,000. The Abu Safra family, which is a part of the Romailat tribe, is famous for rearing and breeding the best Arabian horses in the world. The Meliti family, which is a part of the Torabeen tribe that lives in Abu Neitoon, is famous for raising the best breed of camels – called the "pure camels" – known for their speed, strength and endurance. They are used for long-distance traveling as well as racing.

People around the world have customs unique to themselves. The Bedouin of Sinai are no exception. For instance there are "saintly ancestors" and "bad ancestors." In the desert the Bedouin have many graves of "saintly ancestors," which they sanctify, swear by, give votive offerings to, and visit each year on different occasions. They light the graves and give slaughtered offerings: For the prophets they slaughter a camel, and for the ancestors they offer the head of a lamb or a goat. There are also "prophet ancestors," who are basically the Prophet Aaron, and the good Prophet Abu Taleb, and the Prophet Moses. These exist in the Tor region. Just as they have the good, saintly ancestors, the Sinai Bedouin have bad ancestors on whom they pour swear words and insults, throwing stones at their graves. There is Hood and there is Amri, the bad ruler in the Upper White Valley, 10 miles from Awga'a on Ghanza Road.

Offerings to the sea are a practice of the Wararka, the Bayaseen and the Akharsa tribes of the Arish Desert. The offerings of slaughtered animals, derived from heathenish ritual, is an annual event after spring. They visit the sea with their tents, bringing their horses, camels and cattle. They wash them in the sea, then slaughter some, throwing animal heads, legs and skin into the water saying: "This is your dinner, O Sea!" They then cook the rest of the meat, feeding themselves as well as passersby.

The Sawarka tribe also visits the sea, but without celebrating. The Alaha celebrates for one day, from evening till the following morning, and slaughter near the seashore between Rafah and El-Arish. The Bayadeyeen and the Akharsa tribes, who live in Kateya, descend to the seashore at the Mohammadeya, near Farma, and carry out a magnificent celebration, with horse and camel racing, and with women trilling cries of joy for three days.

South of Rafah well, there are two closely linked trees called the *Makroonatan*, or literally, the Twins. Each has a branch that bends to the ground, and inside these branches is a hollow where one can find small pieces of old and new coins, nails, beads, and lentil seeds. On the branches of both trees the Bedouin hang oil lanterns.

Over 50 years ago, the great researcher Naom Shair determined that the Bedouin women honor the two trees, giving them votive offerings; and when they come to visit, they put something of themselves in the trees, lighting them up with lanterns as the Bedouin do when they visit the sacred, saintly ancestors.

"Whitening" refers to the tradition of putting a white flag over someone's house, instead of stoning him; while "blackening" refers to placing a black flag as a symbol of ugliness. A man might call for help from another tribe to prevent some evil, and if the two tribes begin a war or if two men begin a fight, one of those present says, "I throw my face, or the face of so and so, between us!" both conflicting parties should

immediately stop fighting. Why? The face has great sanctity. If war continues after "throwing" the face, the owner of that face would say: "So and so cut my face."

He then asks his enemy to accompany him to the *mashad*, or judge; and if refused, he brings four witnesses and takes his enemy's camels until the latter succumbs to the judge. The *mashad* can sentence the accused to pay from two to forty camels, depending upon the degree of the "cut face." The *mashad* also may sentence him to cut two centimeters of his tongue, thus saving a number of camels. Note: a Bedouin never forgets an evil done to him, nor a good. He keeps his gratitude and even hands it over to his sons as inheritance.

The Bedouin community does not know prisons. Most sentences, according to Bedouin tradition, are in the form of monetary fines, with the camel considered the primary currency. A thief must pay four times the amount of stolen goods to the owner, once the theft is proven beyond a shadow of a doubt.

When the Bedouin sees the half moon every month, he has to sing. They congratulate each other for its appearance, one by saying: "Blessed be your month," while the other answers, "For us and you."

Here are some of the Bedouin customs: *wigdan* is an expression of something that is instinctive, coming from deep inside man's soul, heart and mind. It is a call. The *wigdan* of people, which literally means sentiments, is their poetry, their dancing, their stories and myths, lessons and sermons.

Al Heda is a song, which expresses happiness for a newborn, for circumcision, and for marriage. It also praises spring and traveling, especially traveling on pilgrimage and returning from it.

Al dahia is the best entertainment for Bedouin in their deserts. When the Bedouin meets for the *dahia*, the singers stand in one line, and among them there is one poet or more known as the *beda'a* who improvises poetry. In front of them there is one woman called the *hashya*, dancing with a sword.

Singers begin by repeating "*dahia, dahia*" several times as they clap with their hands and shake their heads. The *beda'a* begins to improvise, and whenever he says one verse, everyone sings a previously learned chorus as they clap their hands and move their heads to the left and right, walking towards the *hashya*. The *hashya* backs in front of them as she dances their dance, until they reach the field; and then they sit down with their legs crossed beneath them; the *hashya* does the same, and they sing for a while. The men then retreat slowly and the *hashya*, still facing them, follows them till they return to their initial place, where they begin dancing as they had done before.

There are many proverbs among the Bedouin of Sinai. Here is a small sampling: *Protect the old, even if the new makes you richer. He who does not know the eagle, grills it. Children are either trade, compensation or loss. God bless the obedient woman, the fast horse, and the big house. Prophesy for the murderer with murder, and the adulterer with poverty. The seller is greedy, and the buyer a thief. No head can wear two fezes. Organized lies are better than scattered honesty. Money that is collected in honesty, the devil takes half of it; whereas money that is collected in dishonesty, the devil himself is its owner.*

After discussing the role of camels in all aspects of their lives – marriage, food, clothing, and the market, including trade, industry, distinctive habits and

Opposite page:
Shepherd women and their animals enjoy the beach at El-Arish.

customs, and their emotions in popular proverbs, or in a dance or a song, there then comes the judiciary and the *shari'a* or law.

As in other areas of Bedouin life, the camel is again one of the most important components of Bedouin law and the common factor in all its articles and items. Let us look at the judiciary council, and how customs are applied there. The judiciary is staffed by a number of special men who judge according to Bedouin traditions and customs. They are usually different types of men: the Great Arabs whose role is reconciliation, based on the lack of witnesses, or based on the magnitude of the consequences of an unpeacefully resolved conflict. They are usually old and wise men. The *mashad*, otherwise known as the *masmaoodi*, referring to the Maseed tribe in El-Arish, judges critical personal matters, such as "face cutting," blackening, matters of honor, or personal insults. The *kasas* is the penal judge, or the judge of wounds. He defines the punishment for every wound according to its length, width and place. He is usually from the Palm districts, in El-Arish, Tor, and from the Kararsha and Mazeena tribes. The *akabi* is a marriage judge, judging in matters of divorce, dowry, dishonor. He is called as such because he is from the Bani Akbi tribe, most of whom are judges. *Al zeiadi* is the judge of camels.

Al mubshe is the judge of crimes that have no witnesses, and he judges the accused with fire, water or by visions. He burns a copper rod on the fire and rubs his palm over it three times. He then orders the accused to wash his tongue with water in front of two witnesses. The accused places the hot rod in his mouth and shows it to the *mubshe* and to witnesses. If they see the fire on his tongue, the *mubshe* makes a judgement against him, for if the accused is guilty, his tongue dries out, and the fire therefore burns his tongue. The *mubshe* also may take a copper pot, asking those present, including the accused, to sit in a circle. They utter certain prayers over the pot, and they claim that the pot moves alone. If the accused is guilty, the pot stops in front of him; and if he is innocent, the pot stops in front of the *mubshe*. With vision, the *mubshe* thinks deeply of the accused then goes to sleep, visualizing the criminal in front of him in a dream. When he awakes, he passes sentence.

Naoom Shokeir, who wrote one of the first books on Sinai, says: "In the entire peninsula, I have not seen except one single *mubshe*, who is Sheikh Amer Ayyad from the Ababda tribe, who inherited it from his father Ayyad, and his uncle Oweimar, and I saw him in Rafah in 1906, and therefore I talked about him."

The Bedouin court system consists of the same levels of classification as the Egyptian courts: The court of first instance, the court of appeal, and the court of cassation. The court consists of three of the great, wise Arabs – one *monshed* or singer, one *kasas*, one *okbi* or executioner – three from the Zayadi tribe, three from the Daribi tribe, and one *mubshe*. It is a true legal system, although oral and unwritten. Crimes of the highest degree are murder, theft, insults, kidnapping girls, burning other people's crops, trespassing, covering up wells, not paying debts, and making war. If two tribes wish to reconciliate, their elders meet, and they spill blood for everyone whose murderer is unknown. If the murderer is known, his sentence is set. Stolen money is not returned. Reconciliation happens through oaths and vows.

Egyptian courts have begun operating in Bedouin areas, but both systems currently are applied.

Camels, being the largest currency known in the Sinai Desert, are used in punishments. Rape of a virgin from the male's same tribe calls for a fine of six camels, while the rape of a widow of another's tribe is only two camels, provided the widow files an immediate complaint. If she does not, the punishment is a small camel.

Polygamy and early marriages abide among the Bedouin. A man is required to act fairly among his wives, providing each of them with a tent, and coming to each of them one night. If he neglects one of the women's turn, she ties one knot into a long thread. Every night he neglects her, she ties another knot until her patience is tried. Then she takes the knotted thread to her family, which will take it to the judge. He will order the husband to pay one camel for every night he abandoned his wife.

Camel punishment is severe.

Below:
An old Bedouin woman sits cross-legged.

Following pages:
A fjord cuts into the hilly coastline of the Gulf of Aqaba near Taba.

Sinai's Underwater World

by Ayman Taher

No book on Sinai would be complete without describing the beauty of El Baher Ahmer – the Red Sea. Its presence extends deep into Sinai through the two long, narrow fingers that hold the peninsula between them, the Gulf of Suez and the Gulf of Aqaba.

There are many theories to explain how the Red Sea earned its name. There is the reflection of the red hue at sunset from the surrounding mountains, the dust carried onto her waters, red tides, reddish colors of the fish and its coral. The beautiful mountains of South Sinai formed over two million years ago are unique and sacred, yet barren, rugged and harsh. They have a close resemblance to the barren landscape of the moon. The sun flushes the mountains with shades of red that change from a pale, hushed rose at sunrise to a warm red at sunset.

The Red Sea is the only enclosed coral sea in the world and reaches depths of 2,000 meters. The waters are very clear, with a visibility that is unparalleled anywhere else in the world, mainly due to the mild currents and the absence of industrial and other pollutants. The excellent visibility and clear water permit light to reach great depths, allowing life to be sustained and permitting large varieties of corals to flourish.

Surrounded by desert, the region has a hot climate. The climate and absence of any rivers feeding the sea with fresh water makes the Red Sea one of the saltiest seas. Its salinity reaches up to four percent.

Ras Mohammad, at the southern tip of the peninsula, is internationally recognized for the beauty of its coral reefs. Nearby Sharm el-Sheikh commands a hilltop view from Ras Mohammad to the Straits of Tiran. While some may debate whether Australia's Great Barrier Reef or the Gulf of Aqaba is the world's greatest underwater diving site, the accessibility of the coastline of South Sinai to Europe and the Middle East makes it an appetizing playland for millions of tourists.

For these reasons and more, the Red Sea is the Mecca of underwater photographers. As a photographer, my pleasure is never-ending. New dimensions are opened up through my lenses. A fairy-tale world full of little creatures is captured through the macro lens. What I see with the naked eye takes a different dimension through the wide-angle lens. I can only but try to capture and record part of this kaleidoscopic world and bring home to you what is of greatest revelation to me.

Leaving behind the harsh and arid wilderness of the mountains of Sinai, I slide into the depths of the magical universe of marine life. Embraced by the wonderful

Opposite page:
Ganiopora coral of the Pontidae *family is the most significant contributor to coral-reef growth.*

Pages 138-139:
Diaphanous Dendrophyllid *coral seem to glow in a nighttime dive.*

Pages 140-142:
A Hawkfish (Cirrhitidae) *swims through a fan coral.*

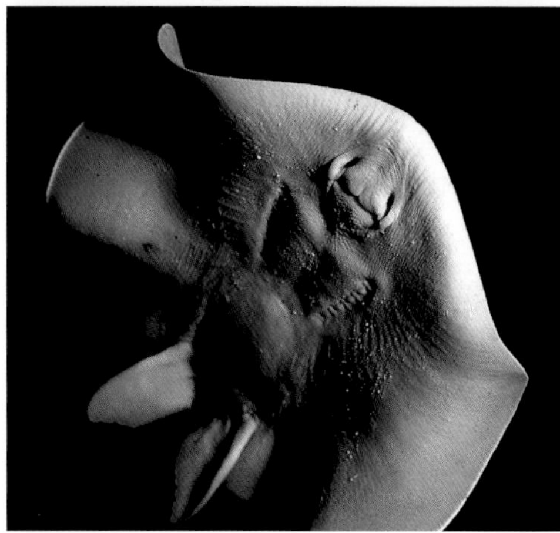

Top: *Lionfish (*Pterois-volitans*)*
Below: *Electric ray (*Torpedo-sinusperici*)*.

feeling of gliders when gravity ceases to exist, I am suspended in a world that is unparalleled in its beauty. One becomes part of this spellbinding environment, relating to one and all sea mammals, especially the dolphins. Only the mechanical sound of the bubbles brings home the reality that I am the outsider.

Exploring the exquisite secrets of the sea, one witnesses the sheer extravagance of colors, shapes and forms within a few square meters. From the tiny detailed fan coral, to the huge bulky brain coral. From the colorful soft coral to the colorless stony fire coral. The grace of the Spanish dancer (*Hudibranch*) unfolds; the ugly venomous stone fish stands out. You cannot but become deeply involved in the life of the reef.

When underwater, part of me is tuned to the different, changing moods of the sea. From morning to dusk to nightfall, the changes in colors and shapes are startling. Dusk provides the greatest fascination to the eye of the beholder. It is a time of reunion when the fish come from open waters to the reef. At nightfall the mood changes. It is a time when creatures disappear and others appear. The parrot fish puts the cocoon around her eyes as a sort of protection. The Dendrophyllid opens up at night, and the feather stars emerge in large numbers to feed along the edge of the reef.

One is astounded by the contrast between the hot, barren desert and the cool, clear, blue waters of the Red Sea teeming with life. It is a unique experience for a snorkeler or diver to don his mask in the midst of this hot, harsh desert scenery and then, suddenly enter a magical underwater world brimming with beautiful living creatures.

The Red Sea contains one of the richest of marine fauna, with more than 1,000 species of fish, ranging from whale sharks – the world's largest fish measuring up to 32 feet – to minuscule crustaceans. Ten percent of the most attractive coral-reef fishes are endemic species to the Red Sea and the Gulf of Aqaba.

The world of underwater photography is filled with many fine photographers, who carefully document and categorize the underwater world they encounter. I feel it imperative to capture the character of each living creature in its watery environment. There is an intangible spirit in Ras Mohammad that I have tried to harness in the photographic image: to show the natural beauty of this special place in a unique way that allows the soul of the sea to speak to us directly, to connect on an emotional level rather than on an intellectual or scientific one. I hope I have accomplished this in my works.